Fixing Truancy Now

Fixing Truancy Now

Inviting Students Back to Class

Jonathan W. Shute and Bruce S. Cooper

ROWMAN & LITTLEFIELD
Lanham • Boulder • New York • London

Published by Rowman & Littlefield
A wholly owned subsidiary of
The Rowman & Littlefield Publishing Group, Inc.
4501 Forbes Boulevard, Suite 200, Lanham, Maryland 20706
www.rowman.com

16 Carlisle Street, London W1D 3BT, United Kingdom

British Library Cataloguing in Publication Information Available

Library of Congress Cataloging-in-Publication Data

Shute, Jonathan.
  Fixing truancy now : inviting students back to class / Jonathan Shute and
Bruce S. Cooper.
    pages cm
  Includes index.
  ISBN 978-1-4758-1005-9 (cloth : alk. paper) — ISBN 978-1-4758-1006-6
(pbk. : alk. paper) — ISBN 978-1-4758-1007-3 (electronic) 1. School
attendance—United States. 2. Minorities—Education. 3. Children with social
disabilities—Education—United States. 4. English language—Study and
teaching—Foreign speakers. I. Cooper, Bruce S. II. Title.
  LB3081.S48 2014
  371.2'94—dc23   2014018553

Printed in the United States of America

To Dennis O'Keeffe,
a champion for fixing truancy now.

Contents

Chapter One

Understanding and Defining Truancy

Truancy continues to be a staggering problem throughout our country, one that plagues our schools. As Arne Duncan (current U.S. secretary of education) and Kamala D. Harris (current California attorney general) recently reported, "Millions of desks sit empty in elementary school classrooms because of truancy each year, costing schools billions of dollars, wasting public resources and squandering one of the country's most precious resources: its young people" (Duncan & Harris, 2013, p. 1).

Our young people are our country's most precious resource, and since truancy has been a crippling problem for decades, it behooves us to dig more deeply into the problem than we have heretofore. No amount of effort should be avoided in helping our young people find ways to reconnect with learning. Obviously, we either haven't understood the magnitude of the problem or grasped how to deal with it successfully. We must find creative ways to resolve this problem.

TRUANCY DEFINITION

The word *truancy* conjures up images of juvenile delinquents across the country skipping school to commit crimes. Historically, truancy has meant the act of intentionally skipping school without a legitimate excuse from a parent or guardian. The number of days a student can miss school before being considered "truant" is a number determined by individual states (Seeley, 2006, p. 1).

Perhaps the negative lens through which we have viewed truancy comes from the word itself. *Truant* as a noun has its origins in the 12th

1

century Old French word *trougant*, a "beggar, vagabond, or rogue." The Welsh used the term to mean *wretch* or *wretched*. And the Spanish, *truhan*, means *buffoon*. Later in the mid-15th century, a truant was "one who wanders from an appointed place" (etymology online dictionary).

The origin of the word fits nicely with the connotation we give the word today: *rogue*, *buffoon*, and *wretch*. However, to solve the truancy problem, we must step back and ask: is the place from which these buffoons wander a good place? If it were a good place, would they wander away from it by the millions?

In recent years, new assertions have been made to the effect that in most cases of truancy, the juvenile delinquent image is wrong. The majority of truants are not social deviants and juvenile delinquents; rather, they are students who truant as a rational decision (i.e., students who will not tolerate subjects that seem to them inadequate or teachers who seem poorly prepared, boring, or both).

In other words, these rational decision-makers are "wandering" from the appointed place because in their perceptions that appointed place is not beneficial for them. Of course, school officials with history on their side would argue with this assertion. In truth, they have a difficult time changing their perception of truancy—they cling to the old and established notion about truancy as a deviant behavior. However, research shows these truants make up the small minority of overall truants.

We should consider truancy in a much larger sense, that is, students who deliberately miss certain classes. And if we associate the truancy problem with the much larger percentage of truants who miss *class* as opposed to *school*, our solutions will, in fact, bring both groups—class and school truants—back to school.

The traditional view of truancy was confined to only those students who skipped entire days of school without excuse. But what about those students—and research shows there are far more of them—who arrive at school and then skip certain classes during the day? The limitation of the traditional view of truancy is not applicable today.

The act of truancy that involves skipping one or more classes after arriving at school must be included in the definition. Including these class-skipping students into the truancy definition will greatly expand the breadth of the truancy discussion and more precisely help us get at the heart of the matter. We must expose the real reasons behind the problem, thereby giving us tools to deal with it.

Searching for a viable solution requires a clear definition of the problem. Perhaps part of the problem with the traditional view of truancy stems from the lack of a clear term. We have allowed the term *truant* to limit and cloud our perceptions. For example, should we combine students who skip three classes a month into the same category as those students who skip three days a month? Some states, now, are including tardies and missed individual classes into their definitions. For example, California defines truancy as being "absent or tardy by more than 30 minutes without a valid excuse on three occasions in a school year" (Harris, 2013, p. 1).

In this book, we use the word *truancy* to mean both those students who skip entire days of school and those students who skip one or more classes after they arrive at school. We are not the only educators who define truancy this way. School districts across the country are forced to account for those students who skip class without a legitimate excuse, and, fortunately, many of these school districts, like in the state of California, are including them in the truancy discussion.

The truancy problem is not confined to Caucasian students. The ethnic minority and English language learner (ELL) populations have seen tremendous growth patterns over the past three decades in the United States and, subsequently, in our schools. With this increase, problems arise in how to best service these children who are truant. Socioeconomic issues surface, cultural adjustment problems emerge, and with the increase of ethnic minority children entering our schools, English language issues will surface. These issues will compound the general problem of truancy that we will have to face in our nation's schools.

BRIEF HISTORICAL SUMMARY

Truancy became a major problem in the United States with the advent of compulsory education (Smith, 1979, p. 1). One might claim that truancy is built in to the very phenomenon of mass and compulsory education, in that people may be more likely to rebel against something that is forced upon them.

In the early years of truancy and up to World War II, truancy was perceived as mainly a psychological problem. After all, because compulsory education is such a good prospect for students, and since a person cannot possibly obtain too much schooling, anyone who would purposely absent himself or herself from school must have psychological problems. The blame for truancy was laid upon the psychological dysfunction of the truant and *away* from the school.

Since the 1960s, however, the focus of the investigation of school attendance has become less psychological and more social. If a student is absent without excuse from school, sociological issues such as family problems, poverty, or involvement in gangs are to blame. With this societal view toward truants, the answers for the cause of truancy center on the social aspects of the truant, which continues to keep any blame *away* from what is happening in the school learning environment.

Undeniably, some truants fit the traditional view and are absent from school because they choose to be and are, in fact, deviants and delinquents. Evidence shows that oftentimes crimes are committed by youth who should be in school. "As a risk factor for delinquent behavior in youth, truancy has been found to be related to substance abuse, gang activity, and involvement in criminal activities such as burglary, auto theft, and vandalism" (Baker, Sigmon, & Nugent, 2001, p. 1).

Another frightening report states, "Of the 85 juveniles convicted of murder in New York State between 1978 and 1986, 57.6% had a history of truancy" (Grant et al., 1992, pp. 459–72). In addition, reports state that all criminals started their lives of crime with truancy.

The California School Board Association Task Force explains that "95% of those considered juvenile offenders, such as burglars, shoplifters and vandals had started their deviant activities as truants" (Smith, 1979, p. 13). As we read statistics such as the aforementioned, we must be cautious. Even if it were true that all criminals were truants, is it rational to assume all truants are criminals? Aristotle warned us of the dangers of such reasoning 2,500 years ago, with his famous observation that "while all men are animals, not all animals are men."

So, while we acknowledge that some truants are juvenile delinquents, we strongly assert that these individuals are a small percentage of the overall students who truant from school and class, and the continual focus on the criminal, social, and psychological reasons impedes progress toward a viable solution of this tremendous problem.

The U.S. Department of Education's *Manual to Combat Truancy* opens by saying, "Truancy is the first sign of trouble; the first indication that a young person is giving up and losing his or her way. When young people start skipping school, they are telling their parents, school officials and the community at large that they are in trouble and need our help if they are to keep moving forward in life" (U.S. Department of Education, 1996, p. 1).

While helping the truant is the goal, this underlying tone keeps us mired in the viewpoint that the truant is a wayward, lost soul in trouble. With this view toward truants, the blame and the answers for truancy center *away* from the school. Our aim here is to portray truancy as an indication of the dysfunctional or malfunctioning state of our schools. A number of educators agree, saying that the dropout rate and truancy rate "could be more adequately described as running away from school, fleeing school, escaping school" (Latham, 1998, p. 59).

With this alternative view of truancy, we are free to wonder if what is happening in our classrooms might be contributing to truancy. Again, while it is, of course, true that some truants are juvenile delinquents and up to no good, and since it is true that a variety of social, economic, and psychological dynamics are at work, we must include in the truancy discussion the possibility that curriculum and pedagogy are also to blame.

THE MAGNITUDE OF THE TRUANCY PROBLEM

A few statistics are in order to establish the magnitude of the truancy problem. The extent of the problem is difficult to capture since in the past very little national data on truancy existed. However, the No Child Left Behind Act has required states, beginning with the 2005–06 school year, to keep track of truancy data, but states are not required to make these data public, and, unfortunately, many states do not (Seeley, 2006, p. 2).

Fortunately, some data are available, which show that the problem of truancy has remained consistently high over the past three decades. In 1973 and in 1976, the National Association of Secondary School Principals rated poor attendance as their most perplexing problem (Smith, 1979, p. 1).

In 1979 it was reported that 2.5 million students were absent on any given day across the United States (Smith, 1979, p. 8), and during the 1996–97 school year, student absenteeism, tardiness, or class cutting was

one of the three discipline issues most often cited by public school principals (National Center for Education Statistics, 1998). "In New York City
about 150,000 out of 1,000,000 students are absent daily. . . . The Los
Angeles Unified School District reports that 10 percent of its students are
absent each day . . ." (DeKalb, 1999, p. 1).

Sadly, we now know truancy is rampant in elementary schools. As we
noted in the beginning of this chapter, "About 1 million elementary school
students in the state [of California] were truant—defined in California as
three or more unexcused absences or tardinesses—during the 2012–13
school year" (Duncan & Harris, 2013, p. 1). The high school truancy
situation is as perilous. In 1992 the federal government surveyed nearly
16,000 high school seniors and found that 91% admitted to cutting school
(Cooper, 1998, p. 1).

Studies have indicated and continue to show that truancy is a crippling problem for educators. The sad fact is that these few statistics, in
many cases, do not factor in truancy from class after students arrive at
school. However, we must applaud some states—namely California and
Colorado, among others—for making their truancy data public, which is a
wonderful step in truancy prevention efforts, acknowledging their willingness to tackle this problem openly.

A major research project was conducted in the western United States in
2005 that did include the class truancy element. In this study, over 2,700
students were surveyed and nearly 65% admitted to being truant in the two
months prior to the survey. In addition, over 71% of the ethnic minority
students were cutting class and school, and over 70% of the English language learners truanted (Shute, 2009). More details on this study and other
important truancy information will be presented throughout this book.

Problems arise when reporting truancy data. For example, many students are truant on the day surveys are given in school and thus cannot
respond to survey instruments. In addition, attendance statistics across
some districts will mask truancy statistics at specific schools within the
district. In New York City, "at 96 of the 366 middle schools, more than
30 percent of youth were chronically absent during the 2007–2008 school
year, but the average school-wide attendance rates for each grade during
the same year were at least 90%, a target viewed by many schools to be
acceptable" (Yeide & Kobrin, 2009, p. 1).

And, of course, students who have already dropped out of school will not be included in the truancy data. Unfortunately, truancy rates are not only astronomically high, but it is quite obvious that they are not all that accurate in showing the real magnitude of the problem.

IMPACT OF TRUANCY

Many segments of our society suffer from the truancy epidemic. The Office of Juvenile Justice and Delinquency Prevention named truancy reduction as one of its national priorities for 2003 (Yeide & Kobrin, 2009, p. 3). As a country, the deleterious impact on the productivity of the American labor force that truancy unarguably brings must take its toll, since businesses pay to train uneducated workers.

At the individual state and district level, the financial losses are staggering. Each year, individual schools lose hundreds of thousands of dollars of federal and state funds that are based on daily attendance figures. In California, the estimated financial loss in school districts was $1.4 billion during the 2010–11 school year (Harris, 2013, p. 23).

The 2005 United States Census Bureau reports that the nation's average yearly spending in 2003 to educate one child was $8,019—the District of Columbia had the highest spending rate at $13,328 per child while Utah had the lowest per pupil expenditures of all states at $4,860 per child (Toomer-Cook, 2005).

In Utah, 77,140 students attend one school district and, of those, 17,787 are high school students (Jordan School District). Multiplying this cost, for this district the state pays more than $86 million to educate these students, in the lowest spending state of the nation. Expand this to the thousands of school districts across the country, and this amounts to an almost unimaginable expense. Given the estimated truancy levels in our country, the financial waste is, without question, monstrous.

Americans are not alone in this dreadful waste. In the United Kingdom, the government spent £885 million over the past seven years on initiatives focused on fighting absenteeism. The country's frustration is summed up by Edward Leigh M.P., chairman of the House of Commons' committee of public accounts, when he said that he was disappointed that the Department of Education and Skills had "missed by a mile its targets to reduce truancy" (Lepkowska, 2005, p. 1).

Taxpayers carry the burden through the cost of court time, personnel, and fees paid to attorneys that represent schools in truancy hearings. Taxes must be higher to pay for law enforcement and welfare costs for truants who drop out and eventually end up on welfare. And, of course, the people who are affected the most are the students. Absenteeism leads students to fall behind and is detrimental to achievement, graduation, and employment potential.

HOPES FOR OUR FUTURE

Even though the truancy problem is bleak, we declare hope: hope for teachers and school officials, and for parents and students. This book will offer hope by explaining why we have such a huge truancy problem, describing the details of the problem and discussing why schools (namely the teaching and pedagogy that are occurring in our schools) must accept much of the blame. Fortunately, if schools accept this blame, effective teaching and pedagogy can be improved, thereby reducing the truancy problem.

We realize many teachers will likely discard this book after reading that last paragraph. If not, please let us clarify. Many teachers and administrators are hardworking, conscientious, and desirous for positive change. They are inviting, warm, and patient with many truant students. They strive to implement effective teaching practices to engage, encourage, and develop students because they know that through effective pedagogy, not by coercion and force, they can and should keep our students in school. Such is the message of this book.

However, others like us realize that many teachers and administrators either do not have the same outlook on effective curriculum and pedagogy or do not know how to implement effective curriculum and pedagogy. After understanding the real reasons for truancy, we can meaningfully explore how teachers, school leaders, parents, and, most importantly, students can work together to embrace the truancy challenge and work toward its resolution.

THIS BOOK

This book picks up where our earlier one, *Truancy Revisited* (Guare & Cooper, 2003) left off, looking at the three basic types of *truancy*: (1) skipping school altogether, (2) cutting classes but attending school, and (3) dropping out of school (for long periods of time or permanently).

We describe the supposed "causes" of truanting from three important perspectives. First, the truant's view of why they are cutting school; second, the teachers' perspective since it is often blamed on poor instruction, difficult courses, and lack of teacher help; and, third, the "system" perspective, since it may be the whole educative process that causes teachers to treat students badly, stimulate kids to cut school or class, or lead them to leave the system altogether.

To expect 55 million children ages 5–19 in the United States to all attend school for some 180-plus days per year for 13 or more years may be a dream that doesn't readily come true. As the largest, most complex, and changing social program in the nation, if not the world, one can expect some kids to drop out, not show up, and quit. What works educationally for youngsters in grades pre-kindergarten through about fifth grade may not fly for adolescents, and beyond.

No one knows who to blame since the problem is so complex. And unless the schools, classrooms, and process are made more attractive to children and more engaging for all, we are likely to see the cutting, skipping, and dropping out to continue. Making the transitions from childhood to preadolescence to adolescence—being perhaps some of the most difficult—and from being a little child through postpuberty, teenage years, and beyond are hardly considered as schools teach, help, and counsel students.

Each cohort blames another or two. Thus parents are likely to blame the schools for not supervising and nurturing their kids, while school administrators may blame parents for not seeing that their children attend school regularly. Teachers may blame the students when they don't come to school regularly.

But blame isn't the answer. Trust, hope, and caring together is what works, and schools, teachers, parents, and governments should collaborate and put energy into working together to make schools more friendly, happy, and attractive so children will want to attend. Truancy is everyone's problem, and everyone involved should take responsibility for getting all children to school, then to classes, and into their work. Learning is critical and fun if family, schools, and kids come together.

Diane Ravitch (2012) suggested these seven steps that can help everyone work together to benefit children, families, schools, and society:

1. Join Parents Across America. Their website is www.parentsacross america.org. This group is made up of parents who want to work together to strengthen public education and restore common sense reforms.
2. Write to your elected officials. Find out whether any congressmen or senators from your state are on the education committee in their House of Congress. . . . Speak up at school and community meetings. Speak up, speak out.
3. Gather a group of teachers, principals, and parents and schedule a meeting with your local legislator, your member of Congress, or your state and local representatives.
4. Run for your school board. Run for elected office in your town, city, community, or state.
5. Vote for candidates who pledge to support public education and fund the needs of children and schools.
6. Invite local civic and business leaders to spend a day in your classroom and school. Invite them to teach for a day.
7. Build alliances between teachers, principals, parents, and the local community to support children and the school. (http://www.diane ravitch.com/action.html)

We must stop blaming and start sharing and saving our schools (SOS), as their leader explained (http://saveourschoolstoday.org/sos-programs/ pillsbury-pedal-power/):

It is my hope that through SOS we can change the culture surrounding education, so everyone takes a vested interest in the success of our most valuable asset—our children. . . . Their hard work and perseverance is something to be admired. It gives me hope—the more opportunities we can provide these children, the more we can place them in a position of leadership, the more we will see them rise to the occasion and be successful.

REFERENCES

Baker, M. L., Sigmon, J. N., & Nugent, M. E. (2001). Truancy reduction: Keeping students in school. *Juvenile Justice Bulletin.* Washington, D.C.: Office of Juvenile Justice and Delinquency Prevention, September 2001.

Cooper, B. S. (1998). Skipping school for fun and profit. *American Outlook.* Hudson Institute (Spring 1998).

DeKalb, J. (1999). Student Truancy. *U.S. Department of Education.* ERIC DIGEST, ED429334. April, 1999.

Duncan, A., & Harris, K. D. (2013, September 20). How California should deal with truancy. *L.A. Times.*

Grant, C. A., Burgess, A. W., Hartman, C. R., et al. (1992). Juveniles who murder. In A. W. Burgess (Ed.), *Child trauma I: Issues and research* (pp. 459–72). New York: Garland Publishing, Inc. Quoted in National Center for School Engagement. *Truancy fact sheet.* www.schoolengagement.org.

Guare, Rita & Bruce S. Cooper. (2003). *Truancy Revisited: Students as School Consumers.* Maryland: Scarecrow Press, Inc., 2003.

Harris, K. D. (2013). *In school and on track.* Attorney general's 2013 report on California's elementary school truancy and absenteeism crisis. 2013. Office of the Attorney General.

Jordan School District Office of Communications. A guide to Jordan School District. 2005–06. Available from http://www.jordandistrict.org.

Latham, G. I. (1998). *Keys to classroom management.* North Logan, UT: P & T Ink.

Lepkowska, D. (2005, February 4). Truants cost £1.6bn a year. *TES Newspaper.* http://www.tes.co.uk/article.aspx?storycode=2070942.

National Center for Education Statistics. (1998, March). *Violence and discipline problems in U.S. public schools: 1996–97.* NCES 98030.

Online Etymology Dictionary. http://etymonline.com/?term=truant.

Seeley, K. (2006). *Guidelines for a national definition of truancy and calculating rates.* Denver, CO: National Center for School Engagement. www.school engagement.org.

Shute, J. W. (2009). Expanding the truancy debate: Truancy, ethnic minorities and English language learners. In M. Conolly & D. O'Keeffe (Eds.), *Don't fence me in: Essays on the rational truant* (pp. 115–38). Buckingham, England: The University of Buckingham Press.

Smith, L. E. (1979). *Profiles of truancy: A naturalistic study* (doctoral dissertation). Brigham Young University, Provo, UT.

Toomer-Cook, J. (2005, August 16). Back to school: By the numbers. *Deseret Morning News.* http://www.deseretnews.com/article/600156035/Back-to-school-By-the-numbers.html?pg=all.

U.S. Department of Education. (1996). *Manual to combat truancy.* Washington, D.C.: Office of Elementary and Secondary Education. ERIC, ED397526. http://www2.ed.gov/pubs/Truancy/index.html.

Yeide, M., & Kobrin, M. (2009, October 15). *Truancy literature review.* Prepared for U.S. Department of Justice, Office of Justice Programs, Office of Juvenile Justice and Delinquency Prevention, Washington, D.C.

Chapter Two

"Surrounding the Wrong Building"

In the previous chapter, we presented a brief history of truancy and the traditional public perception of it. We also showed the magnitude of the truancy problem and traced the origin of the word *truant* back to its roots—*trougant* (French for *rogue*) and *truhan* (Spanish for *buffoon*)—a person who wanders from an appointed place, the assumption being that the appointed place was a good place, and therefore the wanderer must be a rogue or a buffoon to leave such a place.

Sadly, this view has been the traditional and commonly accepted frame of reference for investigating truancy. The notion that truants are indeed juvenile delinquents and up to no good has dominated society for decades, indeed, since compulsory education became a law.

Thomas Sowell, a brilliant scholar, tells the story of a criminal who was being chased by the Paris police. In his effort to escape, the criminal dashed into a very large building. The police determined that the best thing to do was to surround the building and guard all the exits. Unfortunately, the building had too many exits for the policemen to guard because of the lack of available policemen, so they surrounded the building next door, which was smaller and had fewer exits.

This story, unfortunately, provides a good analogy of what appears to have happened with the traditional approach to truancy. We have surrounded the wrong building by focusing blame on home environment, gangs, and criminal activity. Meanwhile, what may be the real culprit, what is happening inside our schools, has escaped attention.

SUMMARY OF TRADITIONAL REASONS FOR TRUANCY

Since its beginnings, researchers from many disciplines have explained the reasons for the truancy phenomenon. In a broad sense, researchers place the causes for truancy into three generally accepted categories: home and family environment, student, and school.

Home and Family Factors

Studies have long shown that the home and family environment is a major factor in truancy. Regrettably, many unhealthy situations exist within our students' homes and families, including:

1. parental child neglect and/or abuse,
2. lack of parental supervision/family disorganization,
3. parents' drug and alcohol abuse,
4. violence in and around the home,
5. poor parenting skills,
6. parents' physical or mental health problems,
7. parents not knowing attendance laws,
8. parents' lack of support for education or who did not complete education,
9. parent condoned truancy (babysitting, other activities), and
10. low socioeconomic status. (Baker, Sigmon, & Nugent, 2001; DeKalb, 1999; Yeide & Kobrin, 2009).

Obviously, home and family play a role in truancy. When unhealthy situations, like the ones noted previously, exist, school attendance slips in favor of family priorities and, in some cases, family survival.

Student Factors

According to prevailing theories, the student is also to blame for truancy in a variety of ways. Some characteristics of the truant include:

1. a lack of personal and educational ambition,
2. poor academic performance (sometimes due to neurological factors such as dyslexia and special education needs),
3. unmet mental health needs,

4. drug and alcohol abuse,
5. low school attachment/negative attitudes,
6. poor physical health,
7. relationships with other students or the inability to make friends,
8. gang involvement,
9. lack of self-esteem,
10. school-related phobias (when it came time to leave for school in the morning, the children would experience extreme fear and anxiety),
11. inability to make friends with mainstream students or teachers, negative attitudes toward school or teachers,
12. teen pregnancy/parenthood and child care,
13. employment issues,
14. transportation issues, and
15. criminal activity. (Baker, Sigmon, & Nugent, 2001; DeKalb, 1999; Smith, 1979; Trujillo, 2006; Yeide, 2009)

Without doubt, behavioral, physical, and emotional health problems displayed by the student contribute to truancy.

School Factors

We must also face the fact that schools have contributed to truancy in the following ways:

1. lack of clear attendance policies,
2. lack of consistent enforcement of attendance policies,
3. lack of funding to monitor truancy,
4. school size,
5. lack of meaningful consequences,
6. poor record-keeping,
7. not notifying parents/guardians of absences,
8. unsafe school environment,
9. poor school climate,
10. inadequate identification of special education needs,
11. inflexibility in meeting the diverse cultural and learning styles of the students,
12. attitudes of teachers and administrators. (Baker, Sigmon, & Nugent, 2001; Trujillo, 2006; Yeide, 2009).

In addition, some parents value education, although not of the public education variety. They know education is important but believe it can be gained more effectively in places other than public school. For example, the number of homeschoolers is growing. In addition, what about those who agree with homeschooling but lack the funds, expertise, or time?

Ordinary citizens may deeply resent what they regard as the inadequate curriculum and pedagogy in public schools. They may think that school is inadequate as an institution, as are some teachers individually. This group of citizens is quite often neglected as a focus of educational research than many of the students themselves.

Additionally, immigrant children of minority ethnic groups may have weak parental support for education. Some of these parents might appreciate a better education for their children but perhaps feel powerless to provide it. Truants, as we will see, by no means belong entirely to this group of dismissed and educationally forgotten people.

Another group of parents are those who do not value any type of education. These parents perhaps had failed in school themselves and likely did not complete a high school education. Perhaps they believe that they are successful in society and that their children do not need school either. In other words, for them, school is a waste of time.

These reasons for truancy, with variations, continue to prevail in education. They "define" the view of truancy held by educational officialdom. In a 1981 report given by the California School Board Association Task Force on attendance, absenteeism, truancy, and dropouts, a description of the typical truant is: "Joe is academically low functioning; has had difficulty in school for years. His psychological report reads, 'Joe has a general non-caring attitude. He is often defiant to authority figures'" (Smith, 1979, p. 2).

Currently, we have added school and family to the reasons for truancy. The view of the student is the same. "Look at today's truant, and you're looking at tomorrow's criminal," says Assistant City Attorney Terry Bays Smith of Peoria, Arizona (U.S. Department of Education, 1996, p. 3).

CURRENT ONGOING MEASURES TO PREVENT TRUANCY

We now turn our attention to the prevailing traditional strategies that are in use to prevent truancy. Of course, the reasons for truancy will greatly influence the measures attempted to prevent truancy, and since the traditional view of truancy is one where the truant is a juvenile delinquent skipping class and school to commit crime, take drugs, or be with friends, the majority of prevention programs focus on punitive discipline. Searching for answers to truancy in curriculum and pedagogy and other factors within the school has not been attempted.

The *Manual to Combat Truancy* (U.S. Department of Education, 1996) has set the standard for combating truancy. The manual lists steps to deter truancy. We include them here with a short commentary to point out the focus on force and compulsion.

Involve Parents in All Truancy Prevention Activities

Parents play the fundamental role in the education of their children. This applies to every family regardless of the parents' station in life, their income, or their educational background. Nobody else commands greater influence in getting a young person to go to school every day and recognizing how a good education can define his or her future.

For families and schools to work together to solve problems like truancy, there must be mutual trust and communication. Many truancy programs contain components that provide intensive monitoring, counseling and other family-strengthening services to truants and their families. Schools can help by being "family-friendly" and encouraging teachers and parents to make regular contact before problems arise. Schools may want to consider arranging convenient times and neutral settings for parent meetings, starting homework hotlines, training teachers to work with parents, hiring or appointing a parent liaison, and giving parents a voice in school decisions. (U.S. Department of Education, 1996)

While this step sounds somewhat reasonable, the underlying tone is that families and schools must join forces *against* their children. This step advocates mutual trust and communication between families and schools; however, as we shall see in the next step, trust and communication is great until you have a different view from official rule-makers.

Ensure that Students Face Firm Sanctions for Truancy

School districts should communicate to their students that they have zero tolerance for truancy. State legislatures have found that linking truancy to such items as a student's grades or driver's license can help reduce the problem. Delaware, Connecticut, and several other states have daytime curfews during school hours that allow law enforcement officers to question youth to determine if their absence is legitimate. In a few states, including New York, a student with a certain number of unexcused absences can be failed in his or her courses. A Wisconsin judge may, among other options, order a truant to attend counseling or to attend an education program designed for him or her. (U.S. Department of Education, 1996)

Zero tolerance is a wonderful catchphrase, which should be put to the test with serial killers, rapists, racial hate crimes, welfare fraud, and so forth. In other words, the approach here is to assume truants are criminals, worthy of zero tolerance—if school districts force the students back to school, they will not be truant.

Create Meaningful Incentives for Parental Responsibility

It is critical that parents of truant children assume responsibility for truant behavior. It is up to each community to determine the best way to create meaningful incentives for such parents to ensure that their children go to school. In some states, parents of truant children are asked to participate in parenting education programs. Some other states, such as Maryland and Oklahoma, have determined that parents who fail to prevent truancy can be subject to formal sanction or lose eligibility for certain public assistance. Communities can also provide positive incentives for responsible parents who ensure their child's regular school attendance. Such incentives can include increased eligibility to participate in publicly funded programs. Local officials, educators and parents, working together, can make a shared commitment to assume responsibility for reducing truancy—and can choose the incentives that make the most sense for their community. (U.S. Department of Education, 1996)

Many parents, by their own choice or due to circumstances beyond their control, cannot assume responsibility for the feeding and nurturing of their children, let alone force them to attend school. "Positive incentives" for these parents means they must comply or face sanctions. The social variables hindering parents from ensuring their children are in school are also affecting these parents in much more life-threatening ways. Unfortunately, parents' involvement in gangs, crime, drugs, abuse, and poverty seem to render them incapable of tending to their children's educational needs.

Establish Ongoing Truancy Prevention Programs in School

Truancy can be caused by or related to such factors as student drug use, violence at or near school, association with truant friends, lack of family support for regular attendance, emotional or mental health problems, lack of a clear path to more education or work, or inability to keep pace with academic requirements. Schools should address the unique needs of each child and consider developing initiatives to combat the root causes of truancy, including tutoring programs, added security measures, drug prevention initiatives, mentorship efforts through community and religious groups, campaigns for involving parents in their children's school attendance, and referrals to social service agencies. (U.S. Department of Education, 1996)

These stated causes of truancy exclude the school. Where is the possibility that the school is at fault? Until we see the root causes of truancy lie within the school, our efforts will continue to focus on force and compulsion, which, apparently, is the only avenue we know. Continuing from Step 4 in the manual:

Schools should also find new ways to engage their students in learning, including such hands-on options as career academies, school-to-work opportunities, and community service. They should enlist the support of local business and community leaders to determine the best way to prevent and reduce truancy. For example, business and community leaders may lend support by volunteering space to house temporary detention centers, establishing community service projects that lead to after school or weekend jobs, or developing software to track truants. (U.S. Department of Education, 1996)

Here, the manual seemingly turns attention to engaging students in learning. Unfortunately, our excitement at this prospect is short lived. Somehow finding "new ways to engage their students in learning," is really getting businesses to provide better tracking software and offering space for temporary detention centers.

Involve Local Law Enforcement in Truancy Reduction Efforts

> In order to enforce school attendance policies, school officials should establish close linkages with local police, probation officers, and juvenile and family court officials. Police departments report favorably on community-run temporary detention centers where they can drop off truant youth rather than bring them to local police stations for time-consuming processing. When part of a comprehensive anti-truancy initiative, police sweeps of neighborhoods in which truant youth are often found can prove dramatically effective. (U.S. Department of Education, 1996)

Not much ambiguity exists in this item. School officials must join forces with police, probation officers, and court officials. Police sweeps will be the arm of the law to round up truants.

Driven by the perception of truancy advocated in the *Manual to Combat Truancy*, many schools and districts have implemented prevention programs. Each school and district determines their needs to reduce and deter truancy and implements a program modeled after the *Manual to Combat Truancy*.

Our purpose is not to describe every truancy program in the United States but to show a sampling as evidence where the major focus of attention is located, which is mostly on a deficiency in the truant and family. These programs assume the problem of truancy lies within the truant or other sociological aspects of the truant's life, and therefore all efforts, with few exceptions, are aimed at forcing truants back to school, with legal consequences.

We are not criticizing these programs or the hardworking people who create and manage them. Their task is certainly ominous. In fact, many of these programs "work" as measured by the number of truants who are found and put back in school.

In Milwaukee, Wisconsin, "parents, police, and the school system focus on the causes of truancy in the Truancy Abatement and Burglary Suppression (TABS) initiative" (U.S. Department of Education, 1996). The goal is to keep tabs on the children, thus deterring burglary. We can see that even the name of this program links truancy and burglary. "Attendance is taken every period in all high schools. Local police officers pick up truant students and bring them to a Boys and Girls Club for counseling. Parents are called at home automatically every night if their child did not attend school that day. If the parent is not supportive of regular school attendance, then the district attorney is contacted" (U.S. Department of Education, 1996).

The results of this program appear impressive. Of a recent sample, 73% of the students who went through the TABS process were at school the next day. On the 15th day, 66% were in school, and 30 days later 64% were still in school. In addition, daytime burglaries and aggravated battery have decreased since TABS began. Aquine Jackson, director of the Parent and Student Services Division of the Milwaukee Public Schools, says, "I think the TABS program is so effective because it is a collaboration among . . . the Milwaukee Public Schools, the Milwaukee Boys and Girls Clubs, the Milwaukee Police Department, and the County Sheriff . . ." (U.S. Department of Education, 1996).

One program that has received attention is called the THRIVE (Truancy Habits Reduced Increasing Valuable Education) initiative in Oklahoma City, Oklahoma.

> The THRIVE initiative is a comprehensive anti-truancy program that involves an ongoing community partnership of law enforcement, education and social service officials. THRIVE serves truant school-aged youth, who benefit by being removed from negative influences on the street and returned to a safe educational environment. Police take a suspected truant to a community-operated detention center. The centers are staffed by Oklahoma City police officers, a school system staff person on call, and a secretary. The district attorney's office provides additional staffing. Officials assess the youth's school status and release the youth to a parent/guardian or relative. The Oklahoma County Youth Services Agency takes the youths at the end of the day, if a truant's parents cannot be located. (American Bar Association, 2010, p. 13)

The Oklahoma City Police Department reports a drop in daytime burglary rates since THRIVE began.

The Arizona CUTS program (Court Unified Truancy Suppression) was created in response to the growing problem of truancy in Maricopa County. The Juvenile Probation Department identified truancy as a main indicator that youth are at risk. The juvenile, his/her parent/guardian, and a school representative meet at the school. The child is held accountable, parents/guardians are empowered, and communication is improved in the hopes that the juvenile is successful.

To foster and promote long-term changes, consequences are specifically designed to educate and reintegrate the child back into school with the support of school officials. At a CUTS hearing, a juvenile probation officer, a juvenile, their parents/guardian and a school representative come together as a team in order to resolve a truancy citation. To be eligible, the juvenile must admit to being truant and be willing to take responsibility for missing school, which includes discussing the issues surrounding their absences. The probation officer can then assess the case and provide an appropriate consequence. Possible consequences include truancy education classes, community service hours, and tutoring. The juvenile probation officer may also intervene by assigning services such as counseling. Consequences and services are monitored by the juvenile probation officer. The juvenile is held accountable if non-compliant by suspending their driver's license until 18 years of age, or requesting that a court hearing be set. (American Bar Association, 2010, pp. 1–2)

Sadly, the language describing this program uses coercion and force. No real attempt to listen to the student's reasons for truancy is made, nor is an attempt to attack the truancy problem at the source.

The ACT (Abolish Chronic Truancy) program in Los Angeles, California, has been successful. The ACT program is one of the few efforts that intervenes at the elementary school age. This program "places prosecutors in elementary schools to work with administrators, teachers, parents and students to intervene at the very beginning of the truancy cycle. Prosecutors inform parents that it is their legal responsibility to ensure their children attend school and that education is as essential as food, clothing, and shelter in a child's life" (American Bar Association, 2010, p. 3).

If problems exist that interfere with the child's ability to attend school, prosecutors search for community resources to help. The prosecutor can take legal action against the child and the parent/guardian if truancy persists.

The ACT program intervenes as early as possible, preferably in elementary school for a number of reasons: "Truant behavior is not as ingrained at this age as it will later become, the parent of the elementary school–aged child still has control over the child and can, therefore, be held accountable; if intervention occurs later in the child's life, he will have fallen so far behind academically as a result of truancy that getting the pupil back in school will be a matter of winning the battle having already lost the war" (American Bar Association, 2010, p. 3). Unfortunately, the intervention is filled with the perception that we are at battle with our students.

While these are only a sampling of different programs aimed at reducing and preventing truancy, clearly the assumption continues to be mired in the traditional way of thinking—truancy is committed by delinquents. Most of these programs measure their success by reduced crime rates. We must assume these programs represent the best efforts of some administrators with the information they possess with which to make such decisions.

We can be thankful that administrators are taking measures to deal with the truancy problem; however, to truly make effective steps toward solving the truancy problem we must surround the correct building. If we don't, one must wonder if the programs are fixing the truancy problem or simply putting a bandage on it. Research shows that "heavy enforcement of truancy requirements has a short-term effect" (Wilson, 1993, p. 43). In other words, "this get tough method treats the symptoms of truancy, not the causes" (Guare & Cooper, 2003, p. 77).

The *Manual to Combat Truancy* has put the outlook on truancy as a Manichaean battle of good versus evil. The good guy, of course, is the educational establishment, and the bad guy is the truant. The establishment views truancy as the actions of a rebellious student from a dysfunctional home. While, undeniably, some truants fit this profile, and for which these programs "rescue," overwhelming evidence demands a look at the truancy "battle" using a different set of lenses.

A great deal of research indicates that much of the truancy problem is a result of bad curriculum, pedagogy, and other school problems, as has been demonstrated by student comments such as boredom and irrelevant courses. However, students' opinions are not generally taken into consideration because the perception of truancy has not changed. If this perception of truancy by educators, administrators, and policy-makers continues, truancy will remain widespread with tragic consequences.

TRUANCY: A RATIONAL CHOICE

In recent years, new assertions have been made to the effect that in most cases, truancy is not necessarily a "criminal" activity. A minority of writers—specifically Dennis O'Keeffe in *Truancy in English Second-ary School: A Report Prepared for the DFE* and Rita Guare and Bruce Cooper in *Truancy Revisited: Students as School Consumers*—claim that students who truant do so as rational decision-makers who will not tolerate subjects that seem to them inadequate and teachers who seem poorly prepared, boring, or both.

The high truancy levels uncovered by research in the United States, which parallels research in the United Kingdom, demand that a closer look be taken to finding out why the problem of truancy exists in such magnitude. According to the prevailing views, if we equate truancy with juvenile delinquency, 60–70% or more (depending on particular schools) of our youth are juvenile delinquents. We disagree.

To begin, the data on truancy suggest malfunction and dysfunction of our learning environments also contribute to the truancy phenomenon. By "malfunction" of schools, we mean the carrying out of proper activities inadequately. If the school is teaching academic subjects poorly, if it is producing, or not combating, illiteracy or innumeracy, it may be said to be malfunctioning, and truancy may be an index of this.

By dysfunction of schools, we mean that schools may be doing what they ought not to do. Usually, dysfunctionality in school relates more to methods of teaching than to content of lessons. Poor teaching of reading and math must be identified as key weaknesses in schools. We must conclude that malfunction and dysfunction in our schools to some extent lie behind the present pandemic of truancy.

Without question, institutions are set up and managed by humans and do not operate perfectly. For example, many marriages fail, businesses founder, and economies collapse. The implication is not that the institution itself is necessarily bad (though this may sometimes be the case) but that the humans involved are not perfect. Therefore, the institution is subject to error and even decay.

Education in the United States is no exception. The education system, which was set up for the purpose of altruistically educating young people, in some ways has turned into a system, or so some of its critics might maintain, of "polluted politics," which get in the way of sound educational practice. Some issues such as allocation of funds usually take precedence over teaching and learning issues. Large-scale truancy and the closely related behaviors of tardiness and the intentional destruction of lessons seem to be an index, at least, of the partial breakdown of the system.

In reality, these struggles are masked by explaining truancy in terms of characteristics of students and parents, and, if not checked, the educational systems become guilty of hypocrisy. Education is about learning, but unfortunately many educational institutions turn their attention on other issues, pressing as they may be, to escape responsibility brought about by new and relevant research. A better attitude would be this:

> Everybody is unhappy about the way things are. We experiment to make things better, and we argue about what experiments are worthwhile and whether or not those we try are any good. And when we experiment, we make mistakes, and reveal our ignorance, and our timidity, and our naiveté. But we go on because we have faith in the future—that we can make better experiments and better arguments. (Postman, 1995, p. 142)

Research on truancy suggests another view: "one that treats students as thinking, rational decision makers who assess their situation and decide, like other 'consumers' or 'clients,' to 'buy' their units of education (a day or period at a time) or reject school and play hooky" (Guare & Cooper, 2003, p. 2). Truancy is an indication of the continuing decline of our schools. Children are leaving the appointed place to escape. We must ask, why?

If we look closely at what students claim is the cause of truancy, we find boredom, loss of interest in school, irrelevant courses, and bad relationships with teachers; however, "most of the school staff believe[s] truancy to be related primarily to student problems with family and peers" (DeKalb, 1999, p. 1). In addition, "lack of challenging/interesting course work and curriculum was cited by some students as a reason for non-attendance" (Williams, 2012, p. 3). We must focus our efforts on truancy prevention where the real cause lies—inside the school.

The extent of the truancy problem and "evidence that truancy is so widespread—across the sexes, the age cohorts, the grade levels, and the ethnic groups—that deficit, social, and school theories cannot explain adequately the root causes of truancy" (Guare & Cooper, 2003, pp. 2–3). Research shows that the truant is most typically a rationally thinking person making a conscious decision to absent him- or herself from school.

REFERENCES

American Bar Association. (2010). Criminal justice section. *Model Truancy Prevention Programs.* www.abanet.org/crimjust.

Baker, M. L., Sigmon, J. N., & Nugent, M. E. (2001). "Truancy reduction: Keeping students in school." *Juvenile Justice Bulletin.* Washington, D.C.: Office of Juvenile Justice and Delinquency Prevention, September 2001.

Cooper, B. S. (1998, spring). Skipping school for fun and profit. *American Outlook.* Hudson Institute.

DeKalb, J. (1999, April). *Student truancy.* U.S. Department of Education. ERIC DIGEST, ED429334.

Guare, R., & Cooper, B. S. (2003). *Truancy revisited: Students as school consumers.* Lanham, MD: Scarecrow Press, Inc.

O'Keeffe, D. (1993). *Truancy in English secondary schools: A report prepared for the DFE.* London: HMSO.

Postman, N. (1995). *The end of education: Redefining the value of education.* New York: Alfred A. Knopf.

Smith, L. E. (1979). *Profiles of truancy: A naturalistic study* (doctoral dissertation). Brigham Young University, Provo, UT.

Sowell, T. (1992, September). "Public policy and some personal reminiscences." *Imprimis 21*(9) Hillsdale College, Hillsdale, Michigan.

Trujillo, Lorenzo A. (2006). School Truancy: A Case Study of a Successful Truancy Reduction Model in the Public Schools. UC Davis Journal of Juvenile Law & Policy. Vol. 10–1. Winter 2006.

U.S. Department of Education. (1996). *Manual to combat truancy.* Washington, D.C.: Office of Elementary and Secondary Education. ERIC, ED397526. http://www2.ed.gov/pubs/Truancy/index.html.

Williams, L. L. (2012). *Student absenteeism and truancy: Technologies and interventions to reduce and prevent chronic problems among school-age children.* Valdosta State University. http://teach.valdosta.edu/are/Litreviews/vol1no1/williams_litr.pdf.

Wilson, K. G. (1993, April). Tough on truants: Take kids to court to keep in school. *The American School Board Journal.* Board Briefings, p. 43.

Yeide, M., & Kobrin, M. (2009, October 15). *Truancy literature review.* Prepared for U.S. Department of Justice, Office of Justice Programs, Office of Juvenile Justice and Delinquency Prevention. Washington, D.C.

Chapter Three

Truancy by the Numbers

Only a handful of large-scale truancy studies have been done in recent history, especially those that involve asking truants about their truanting behavior. This chapter will bring attention to four of these studies. First, we turn to education in England, which is comparable in structure and approach to the United States. Therefore, research completed in England can be useful to further the cause of education in any country. In addition, other research conducted in British schools for different educational behavioral topics assumes findings to be of value in the United States (Marzano, 2003, p. 31).

As mentioned earlier, the study of truancy by asking students why they truant is a difficult proposition. We must keep in mind that some students will be absent on the day of the survey, and some of those absent students will be truanting. Possibly, when the percentages look stable or are even falling, they could actually be sounding the alarm of a greater problem. The percentages could be stable or falling because more and more students are truanting and are therefore absent on the day we ask them if they truant. More truants are absent, missing the survey, and more nontruants are present taking the survey. The data could show apparent stability while the problem of truancy is actually increasing.

TRUANCY IN ENGLISH SECONDARY SCHOOLS

In September 1991 the British Department of Education financed the largest study of truancy ever done in the United Kingdom. The results of this study were published in a book titled *Truancy in English Secondary Schools: A Report Prepared for the DFE* (O'Keeffe, 1993). This research was perhaps the first to illuminate that the truancy phenomenon was an indication of a problem that exists in the classroom, namely curriculum, methodology, and pedagogy. Perhaps the first of its kind, this study, instead of focusing on numbers of missing students, focused on asking the truants, who were present that day, why they truanted.

This entire study thoroughly explores the truancy phenomenon. For our purposes in this book, the following aspects will be touched upon:

1. frequency of truancy,
2. type of truancy: school truancy, or cutting an entire day of school (referred to as blanket truancy in England), and class truancy, or cutting certain classes after arriving at school (referred to as postregistration truancy in England)
3. like or dislike of school in general, and
4. reasons for truanting.

For the purposes of his research, O'Keeffe focused strongly on class truancy, while at the same time thoroughly investigated school truancy in general. Data were gathered through the administration of a confidential questionnaire, with 45,414 pupils attending the 150 schools that participated in this study. Of these 45,414 pupils, 37,683 completed the questionnaire. Therefore, 7,731 (17%) students were not present at school on the day of the survey.

The researcher notes that without doubt, many of these missing students were absent for legitimate reasons. However, following the results discussed later, one can assume, even minimally, that a third of these students were truanting. That being the case, the data from this research are understatements, and the truancy situation in the schools is worse than the results show.

Even with these students being absent and not completing the questionnaire, this study represents the largest school-based study of truancy to date in the United Kingdom. In our research, we have found no other study of truancy as extensive as the O'Keeffe study.

FREQUENCY OF TRUANCY

The O'Keeffe questionnaire asked students to indicate how often they had truanted in the six weeks prior to this study. A total of 30.5% of the total number of students who participated in the study admitted they truant. Amazingly, 7.2% of the students admitted to some form of truancy either once a week (2.5%), 2–4 times a week (3.2%), or every day (1.5%). Another 5.4% students truant 2–3 times a month, 4.7% truant once a month, and 12.2% truant less often than once a month.

The majority of the truanting occurred at a once a month or greater frequency, and of those truanting more than once a month, the majority occurred at a 2–3 times a month or greater frequency.

The researchers point out that the absence of pupils on the day of the survey inevitably means a greater frequency of truanting in each category. And since the greatest frequencies were in the once a month or more category, the survey data "systematically understates the truancy problem" (O'Keeffe, 1993, p. 32).

TYPE OF TRUANCY

The questionnaire also asked truants which type of truancy they most often engaged in: class truancy, school truancy, or both. The data reveal that class truancy is committed twice as much as school truancy—7% of the truants engaged in class truancy only, 3% in school truancy only, and 20% in both class and school truancy.

The conclusion, as shown later on, is that class truancy shows a particular sensitivity to curricular questions and like or dislike of teachers, subjects, or lessons as opposed to a like or dislike of school in general.

These data are extremely worrisome since the pupils were close to entering "the real world" of work and responsibility. Although the question is outside our findings, such behavior must have implications for the social climate of the workforce. And for our American purposes, let us note that our research data show even more worrying figures. Clearly, these figures establish that truancy is a major problem in England. Year

11 (high school junior) is a crucial year for certification. At the end of this year, important examinations are taken, and students graduate into the workforce, into year 12, or further education and/or higher education.

O'Keeffe comments on the worrisome nature of this phenomenon: "A certain disquiet can be felt in face of the evidence that the academic purposes of the curriculum on offer are being in part rejected by a large minority of pupils" (O'Keeffe, 1993, p. 34). This truancy behavior can only hurt these students' attitudes toward work in their careers for those who start working and their ability to succeed in higher education for those who pursue it.

To take these data one step further for the truants who engaged in class truancy, one question on the survey asked, "In the last half term how often have you skipped lessons?" The data show that 19.4% of the students skip class at least once a week: every day (2.3%), 2–4 times a week (7.5%), or once a week (9.6%). In addition, 13.7% skip lessons 2–3 times a month and 12.2% skip lessons once a month. Interestingly, of the students in this study who skipped lessons, 58.9% "never" leave the building, and 19.4% leave the building "less often."

This total of 78.3% suggests that most class truancy students do not truant to escape school, only to escape certain classes. This result seems to substantiate the contention that most pupils, truants and nontruants, *like* school. They enjoy coming to school. For the truants, they apparently are rebelling against certain classes, not the idea of school.

Even though the highest frequency of truancy is taking place in the "2–3 times a month" or less categories, the lost educational resources and lessons are greatest among the hardcore truants, but still unacceptable for all truants.

For example, 2.3% of the 11,493 truants engage in school truancy every day. Even if these hardcore truants honestly missed only half of the day, this would mean that they miss two and a half days a week. This translates into 90 lessons lost at half term per truant. For 2.3% of the truants (264), 23,760 lessons would be lost. Using the same steps of calculation for the much larger category of "once in a half term" (32.6%, or 3,747 pupils), we find a total of 11,241 lost lessons.

The same holds true for the hardcore class truancy offenders who account for 7,920 lost lessons while the larger "once in a half term" pupils account for 4,402 lessons. O'Keeffe reminds us that these results understate the

magnitude of the findings for two reasons. First, some of the hardcore offenders missed taking the survey, and, second, "it is most unlikely that they
restricted their absences to one lesson a day only" (O'Keeffe, 1993, p. 34).

REASONS FOR TRUANCY

In addition to investigating the frequency and size of the truancy problem,
another main focus of this research was to uncover the reasons why students truant. O'Keeffe contends, and we concur, that truants are rational
decision-makers and not the criminal misfits that the general education
world pegs them to be.

By taking a closer look at the reasons why students truant, we can see
how this hypothesis is sustained. The majority of the truants who completed the survey (67%) stated the avoidance of lessons as their main
motive for truanting. A compelling 49% of the truants gave "to avoid
school" as their reason for truanting. The researchers point out that since
the participants were able to give more than one reason for their truanting,
"it is clear that a great many children reject particular facets of the school
(particular subjects in the curriculum or the homework or coursework
which goes with them, or the people who teach them) rather than the institution as a whole" (O'Keeffe, 1993, p. 53).

As shown, the margins between avoiding lessons, avoiding school,
and other reasons are huge for the class truancy cases only but still large
in the cases of pupils who do both class truancy and school truancy. For
those students who engage in school truancy, the margin is still notice-
able except that in their case, other reasons are almost as important.
O'Keeffe comments,

> It is not that there is no considerable opinion against school among truants.
> Clearly there is. Insofar as pupils are able, however, to distinguish the idea
> of liking/disliking school from the related idea of liking/disliking lessons,
> it is apparent that on their own accounts far more locate their decisions to
> truant in lesson dissatisfaction than in general dislike of school. (O'Keeffe,
> 1993, p. 51)

Of the 49% of truants who reported that they truant to avoid school,
showing a dislike of school, their responses to explain that dislike of

Table 3.1.   Reasons given for dislike of school.

	All Truants (%)	Truants Who Truant Because of Dislike of School (%)
School boring/oppressive	11	23
Particular lesson boring/oppressive	10	20
Schoolwork too hard	4	9
Dislike of teachers	13	27
Already in trouble/detention	1	2

Source: O'Keeffe, Dennis. (1993). *Truancy in English secondary schools: A report prepared for the DFE.* London: HMSO, p. 51.

school included: "school boring/oppressive" (23%), "particular lesson boring/oppressive" (20%), and "dislike of teachers" (27%) (see table 3.1).

Very similar proportions of percentages exist among all truants. In other words, dislike of lessons and teachers combine to create the greatest triggers for truanting among truants, even those who say they truant because of a dislike of school.

For truants who wish to avoid particular lessons, the same idea is borne out. This can be seen in table 3.2.

The truants felt the lessons were irrelevant. Granted, at some point one must question if young students are capable of judging what is relevant or irrelevant knowledge, or if they are capable of deciding what is needed for them to be positive contributors to society when the greater part of life is in front of them. How much freedom they should have to pick and choose subjects of learning is a topic of debate. However, at the very least, these results show that curricular and pedagogic issues are the dominant factors for truanting, and therefore this topic should be debated.

Table 3.2.   Reasons given for avoiding lessons.

	All Truants (%)	Truants Who Truant to Avoid Lessons (%)
Irrelevant lessons	24	36
Dislike of teacher	19	29
Dislike of subject	15	22
Coursework problems	13	19
Difficulty of subject	9	14
Poor teaching	2	3
Bullying	0.7	1

Source: O'Keeffe, Dennis. (1993). *Truancy in English secondary schools: A report prepared for the DFE.* London: HMSO, p. 58.

Table 3.3. Other reasons for truanting in rank order.

	All Truants (%)	*Truants Who Truant for Other Reasons (%)*
Other activities	10	22
Not bothered	6	13
Illness/feeling cold	4	8
General school dislike	2.5	5
Tiredness	2.5	5
Depression	1.8	4
Home problems	1.4	3
Bullying	0.9	2
Peer pressure	0.9	0.9

Source: O'Keeffe, Dennis. (1993). *Truancy in English secondary schools: A report prepared for the DFE.* London: HMSO, p. 60.

OTHER REASONS FOR TRUANCY

Of all the truants, 30% reported that they truanted either exclusively or for reasons other than a dislike of school or lessons. Table 3.3 shows the breakdown of these reasons.

A few other reasons were given to account for truancy. Notably, "peer pressure" was the lowest on the list, and only 2.5% of the truants gave "general school dislike" as a reason. Similarly, only 1.4% of the truants gave "home problems" as a cause.

In conclusion, this study unearthed the magnitude of the truancy problem in the United Kingdom and the reasons for truant behavior by asking the truants themselves. We encourage the reader to explore in more depth this research. In the United States, another study, although not as large, found very similar results.

TRUANCY REVISITED

In 2003 Rita Guare and Bruce S. Cooper published a book titled *Truancy revisited: Students as school consumers.* These researchers, like O'Keeffe, noted that one of the major problems with truancy research is that few researchers have asked truants about their own truanting.

In other words, truancy is a complex interaction between the student, the school, and the classroom—all of which influence students' decision-making processes to attend or not. If the value is there, the customer will, metaphorically speaking, "buy" the product. If the value of school is there, the student will attend. Once schools stop writing off truants as being disturbed, delinquent, or deficient, they will begin to form a clearer picture of truancy. Guare and Cooper have taken this view, and they asked the truants themselves why they truant.

The study examined four main assumptions regarding both types of truancy—class truancy and school truancy. The aim of this research was fourfold:

1. to discover to what degree race, sex, school, or academic standing influences truancy behavior, or if truancy is committed predominantly by youth of all types,
2. to discover if the likelihood of being caught enters into the equation when a student decides whether or not to be absent from school or class on any particular day,
3. to discover if positive home, school, and personal characteristics help a student have better attendance patterns, and
4. to find what helpful action might be taken to boost the student's education while still laying down clear rules and consequences of cutting school or class.

Data were gathered for their research by administering a survey to 230 high school and middle school students, ages 13 to 21. Table 3.4 shows the characteristics of the participants in the study.

As can be seen, 127 males (55.5%) participated in the study compared to 102 females (44.5%). There were 41 eighth graders (17.9%), 45 ninth graders (19.7%), 82 tenth graders (35.8%), 21 eleventh graders (9.2%), and 40 twelfth graders (17.4%) in the study.

The ethnic composition of the Guare and Cooper study is pertinent for our present study in that many of the students were African American at 34.6% (73 students) and Latino at 25.6% (54 students). Anglo-whites comprised 14.2% (30 students), while the "other" category accounted for 23.2% (49 students). The "other" category was assigned to those students who left the ethnicity item blank on the survey. Overall, 62.2% of the students were of nonwhite ethnicity.

Table 3.4.   Characteristics of sample students.

Quality		Frequency	% of Total
a. Sex			
	Male	127	55.5
	Female	<u>102</u>	<u>44.5</u>
	Total	**229**	**100.0**
b. Grade level			
	8th Grade	41	17.9
	9th Grade	45	19.7
	10th Grade	82	35.8
	11th Grade	21	9.2
	12th Grade	<u>40</u>	<u>17.4</u>
	Total	**229**	**100.0**
c. Ethnicity			
	African American	73	34.6
	Latino/Latina	54	25.6
	Anglo-White	30	14.2
	Asian	5	2.4
	"Other"	<u>49</u>	<u>23.2</u>
	Total	**211**	**100.0**
d. English spoken at home?			
	Yes	161	70.9
	Sometimes	45	19.8
	No	<u>21</u>	<u>9.3</u>
	Total	**227**	**100.0**

Source: Guare, R., & Cooper, B. S. (2003). *Truancy revisited: Students as school consumers.* Lanham, MD: Scarecrow Press, Inc., p. 20.

Also significant for our present study was the category of "English spoken at home." As is shown, 70.9% of the participants answered "yes" for this category. A large gap exists before the next category of "sometimes," at 19.8%, and the "no" category was 9.3%. In other words, 29.1% of the participants checked that rather restricted or no English was spoken at home.

Overall, in the Guare and Cooper study a variety of student characteristics existed, which provided a good balance for the data.

As mentioned previously, the age of the participants ranged from 13 to 21. The majority of the students were 14 years old (15.0%), 15 years old (25.2%), 16 years old (22.3%), and 17 years old (17.5%). Overall, 80%

Table 3.5. Comparison of truancy: School vs. class.

	Frequency	% of Total
"Never" Cut Class (N = 227)	73	32.1
"Never" Cut School (N = 221)	135	61.1
"Sometimes" Cut Class	124	54.6
"Sometimes" Cut School	66	29.9
"Often" Cut Class	30	13.1
"Often" Cut School	20	9.1
Total Cutting		
(N = 227) by Class	154	67.8
(N = 221) by School	86	38.1

Source: Guare, R., & Cooper, B. S. (2003). *Truancy revisited: Students as school consumers*. Lanham, MD: Scarecrow Press, Inc., p. 24.

of the participants were either 14, 15, 16, or 17 years of age. This also provided a good balance across these ages that, from the research, appear to be the ages of students who most often engage in truancy behavior.

The first result found in this study was that class truancy occurred more than school truancy. This can be seen in table 3.5.

As is shown, 124 (54.6%) of the participants answered that they "sometimes" cut class, and 30 (13.1%) answered that they "often" cut class. Combining these two categories, we find that 154 (67.8%) of the participants cut class either "sometimes" or "often." By contrast, 66 (29.9%) of the participants admitted to "sometimes" cutting school altogether and 20 (9.1%) said they "often" cut school. This makes a total of 86 (38.1%) subjects that "sometimes" or "often" cut school entirely.

These results affirm that class truancy is more prevalent than school truancy. Guare and Cooper contend that students are "more clinical, almost surgical, in their class cutting." In other words, the students come to school and then cut the classes they deem "unimportant, troublesome, or easily cut" (Guare & Cooper, 2003, p. 26).

These results suggest that contrary to the commonly held notion that truancy is the behavior of social misfits and academic failures, truancy is obviously committed by rationally thinking individuals as well. If it is not, our schools are in dire straits as more than two-thirds of the student population is truant.

Overall, the results of the Guare and Cooper study parallel closely the O'Keeffe study in the United Kingdom. Guare and Cooper found 67.8%

cutting class, while O'Keeffe found 66.1% of the students truanting. Are two-thirds of the high school students in the United States and United Kingdom really the dregs of society? Either the common view of truants needs adjusting or we as a society are in trouble.

Guare and Cooper refuted the long-held view that girls truant less than boys. With regards to class truancy, of the 83 boys who reported truanting, 19 (22.9%) said they cut class "often," and 64 (77.1%) said they cut class "sometimes." In comparison, of the 70 girls who reported truanting, 11 (15.7%) said they cut class "often," and 59 (84.3%) said they cut class "sometimes." Adding these figures together, we see that 83 out of the 124 total boys (66.9%) were truant from class while 59 of the 102 total girls (68.6%) were truant from class.

These results also come very close to the truancy level among boys and girls in the Stoll and O'Keeffe *Officially Present* (1989) study in England.

Of interest are the results when girls and boys were compared with regard to truanting from school entirely. The results show total school cutting for boys at 36.9% and at 40.8% for girls. The data simply do not suggest that boys truant more than girls—indeed the opposite is true.

Another interesting side of this research is truancy by ethnicity. The data show that of the ethnic groups who cut school entirely, either "often," or "sometimes," African American students cut at a frequency of 33.3%, Latinos at 30.8%, Anglo-whites at 48.4%, Asian Americans at 100% (Guare and Cooper are quick to point out that the total number of Asian American participants was only 5, a very small sample size), and "Other" at 46.2%. Table 3.6 shows the breakdown of the truancy percentages of the students from the ethnic minority groups that participated in this study.

We must keep in mind that the "other" category comprises those students who failed to check an ethnic category on the survey. The large number would suggest, had they declared an ethnicity, that the identified categories would have been higher.

When analyzing the data of students who truanted from classes after arriving at school, we see the percentages increase substantially across all ethnic groups. The African Americans reported 64.1%, the Latinos at 60.0%, the Anglo-whites at 87.1%, the Asian Americans at 100%, and the "other" category at 69.2%. Again, the "other" category would obviously raise the percentages across all ethnic groups. And, as reported earlier,

Table 3.6. School truancy by ethnic group.

	African American	Latino/ Latina	Anglo White	Asian American	Other	Total Groups
"I Cut School Often"	11 (44.0%)	1 (6.3%)	4 (26.7%)	3 (60%)	1 (4.2%)	20 (22.7%)
"I Cut School Sometimes"	14 (56.0%)	15 (93.7%)	11 (73.3%)	2 (40.0%)	23 (95.8%)	65 (76.5%)
Total School Cuts	25 (33.3%)	16 (30.8%)	15 (48.4%)	5 (100.0%)	24 (46.2%)	85 (39.5%)
"I Never Cut School"	50 (66.7%)	36 (69.2%)	16 (51.6%)	0 (0%)	28 (53.9%)	130 (60.5%)
Total Sample	75 (100.0%)	52 (100.0%)	31 (100.0%)	5 (100.0%)	52 (100.0%)	225 (100.0%)

Source: Guare, R., & Cooper, B. S. (2003). *Truancy revisited: Students as school consumers.* Lanham, MD: Scarecrow Press, Inc., p. 37.

since Anglo-whites comprised only 14.2% of the total participants, it would seem likely that the African American and Latino group percentages would increase.

The point here is that all groups are deliberately picking and choosing which classes they truant from and are doing so at an alarming level.

Another intriguing aspect to this study is the attention Guare and Cooper have given to how often English is spoken in the homes of the participants. According to the data, 13 of 20 (65%) participants where English is not spoken at home truant from school entirely (school truancy), and 15 of 42 (35.7%) participants where English is only sometimes spoken at home truanted from school entirely.

With these data combined, English not spoken at home and English only sometimes spoken at home, we find that 28 out of the 62 participants (45.2%) truanted entire days of school. Missing from this study are the data that would show how English spoken at home, or the lack of it, affected the participants' class-only truanting behavior.

The final set of data to be looked at here is the relationship between perceived academic standing and truancy. Of the 64 participants who reported an "excellent" (A/B+) rating on themselves, only 4 (6.3%) said they cut class "often," and 36 (56.3%) said they cut class "sometimes." If we combine these two groups, we see that more than half of the "excellent" students, 40 (62.6%), truant "often" or "sometimes."

Out of the 120 students who reported a "good" (B/B-) rating, 15 (12.5%) said they cut class "often," and 68 (56.7%) said they cut class "sometimes." This combines for a 69.2% truancy level among "good" academic students. The percentages for truancy become increasingly greater as academic level goes down. Out of the 38 students who reported a "fair" (C/D) academic standing, 8 (21.1%) said they cut "often" and 20 (52.6%) said they cut "sometimes." Combining these groups together, we find that they truant at an alarming 73.7%.

The figure for the final group, those who reported a "poor" (D-/F) standing, was even higher. Of the 4 students, 3 (75%) said they cut "often" and 0 said they cut "sometimes." As there were only 4 students who took the survey in the "poor" category, it is quite possible that more of these students were truanting on the day of the survey. Although the percentages of truancy increase as the reported academic standing lowers, large amounts of truancy exist among all academic levels. Clearly, the Guare and Cooper study shows that occasional class cutters are not academically challenged students; quite possibly the opposite is true.

HABITS HARD TO BREAK: A NEW LOOK AT TRUANCY IN CHICAGO'S PUBLIC HIGH SCHOOLS

The University of Chicago Consortium for School Research published a large-scale truancy research project. Chicago appears to be an area where research is invited and solutions to the truancy problem are discussed. Truancy is a huge problem in Chicago Public Schools (CPS). For example, in the ten worst schools for attendance, school truancy and class truancy were so bad that the average ninth grader was an extreme truant in at least one major subject by the end of the second semester.

In one school, "the average student missed about half of their instruction time (44 of 90 days) in at least one major subject" (Roderick et al., 1997, p. 6). A major subject is defined, for the purposes of this study, as English, math, social studies, or science. At one school, "class cutting was so common that the median number of days absent from a major subject was twice the number of full day absences" (Roderick et al., 1997, p. 6).

As is generally accepted, no rule determines what constitutes the levels of truancy that pose a threat to learning. The Chicago Public Schools considers a student truant if he or she has even one unexcused absence on any given day. A student is considered a chronic truant if he or she has unexcused absences for more than 10% of the school days. This is 18 of 180 days or 9 days in a 90-day semester (Roderick et al., 1997, p. 3).

This report is very clear in pointing out the two dimensions of truancy, which are cutting full days of school and cutting specific classes. The report characterizes a student as "a good attender if s/he misses 10 or fewer classes or full days a semester, a moderate truant if s/he misses 11–20 classes or full days (2 to 4 weeks) a semester, [and] an extreme truant is if s/he misses 21 days (more than 4 weeks) or more of classes or full days a semester" (Roderick et al., 1997, p. 3).

The research studied 30,000 ninth graders in the Chicago Public Schools during the 1995–96 school year and offers four main findings:

1. A broader conception of truancy is needed.
2. Problem attendance begins early in high school and worsens as the year progresses. Class cutting is widespread.
3. Much of the truancy problem happens because of class cutting, and the truants are often in and around school.
4. Even top students frequently cut class. (Roderick et al., 1997, p. 2)

The first main point is to stress that a broader conception of truancy is needed. The study found that 42% of the "extreme truants" in the second semester had one of three attendance patterns: 26% had 20 or more full-day absences, 10% had 11–20 full-day absences that included class cutting, and 6% attended school somewhat regularly but cut class frequently (Roderick et al., 1997, p. 4). In other words, most of the extreme truancy was because of cutting both full days of school and cutting class. The researchers point out that typically schools identify students as truants if they miss consecutive days of school. "An approach that focuses on consecutive days absent both overlooks students who have very inconsistent attendance yet accumulate many full day absences over the semester, and those who are in school but are cutting classes or are mixing cutting with full day absences" (Roderick et al., 1997, p. 4).

The second finding of this research was that attendance problems begin early and worsen as the year progresses. These data show that as early as the first semester, 50% of the entering ninth graders missed two or more weeks of instruction in a major subject, and 28% missed more than a month of instruction. Of these extreme truants (the 28% who missed more than a month of instruction), 89% ended the year with similar or worse attendance levels. Only 8% slipped into the "moderate truant" category (Roderick et al., 1997, p. 5).

For the 22% of ninth graders who were considered moderate truants in the first semester, the findings were equally bleak. Of these students, almost half (44%) advanced to become extreme truants by the end of the second semester, and 35% stayed moderate truants (Roderick et al., 1997, p. 5).

The frightening finding was that 50% of the ninth graders were "good attenders," but even some of them became truants. Of these students, 11% turned into extreme truants by the end of the second semester, 25% turned into moderate truants, and, sadly, only 64% of the original good attenders stayed good (Roderick et al., 1997, p. 5).

The third main point is that much of the truancy problem happens because of class cutting. The data show that 64% of the ninth grade students truanted from a major subject. Of these, 42% were extreme truants, missing 20 or more classes, and 22% were moderate truants, missing between 11 and 20 classes during the semester.

Comparatively, 47% of the ninth grade students had full-day absences. Of these, 26% missed more than 20 days (extreme truants), and 21% missed between 11–20 full days (moderate truants) (Roderick et al., 1997, p. 5). Clearly, much of the truancy problem in the Chicago Public Schools is cutting class, and it "is happening within and around the school buildings" (Roderick et al., 1997, p. 5).

The fourth main point brought out in this research was that although academically weak students truant, even top students frequently cut class. As was expected, students with weak academic skills were more likely to have truancy problems in high school. Table 3.7 shows the percentage of ninth graders who were moderate to extreme truants by missing 11 or more full days or classes in relation to their academic performance.

The class truancy level is shocking. Over 75% of the students who were 2 or more years below grade level when entering ninth grade truanted from 11 or more classes in a major subject by the end of the second semester. Over 70% of the students who were 1–2 years below grade level were moderate to extreme truants, over 60% of the students 0–1 years below grade level missed 11 or more classes in a major subject area, and, surprisingly, over

Table 3.7.   Poorly prepared students miss the most school,
but even high-achieving students are at risk.

ITBS Eighth Grade Achievement	% of Students Truanting
Percent Missing 11+ Full Days of School (School Truancy)	
On or above grade	23.0
0–1 yrs. below grade	41.0
1–2 yrs. below grade	51.0
2+ yrs. below grade	60.0
Percent Missing 11+ Classes in a Major Subject (Class Truancy)	
On or above grade	42.0
0–1 yrs. below grade	61.0
1–2 yrs. below grade	71.0
2+ yrs. below grade	76.0

*Second Semester, Ninth Grade, CPS 1996.

Source: Adapted from Roderick, M., Arney M., Axelman M., DaCosta K., Steiger C., Stone, S., Villarreal-Sosa, L., & Waxman, E. (1997, July). Habits hard
to break: A new look at truancy in Chicago's public high schools. University
of Chicago. Available from http://ccsr.uchicago.edu/publications/habits
-hard-break-new-look-truancy-chicagos-public-high-schools, p. 8.

40% of the students on or above grade level were moderate to extreme truants by missing 11 or more classes in a major subject area.

The school truancy level is also high. Of the students 2 or more years
below grade level, 60% missed 11 or more days of school. Of the students 1–2 years below grade level, 51% truanted 11 or more days of
school. Of the students 0–1 years below grade level, 41% truanted 11 or
more days of school, and of the students on or above grade level, 23%
missed 11 or more days, making them moderate to extreme truants. The
researchers conclude that "the high rates of absenteeism and course cutting in CPS high schools, even among high-achieving students, point
to an overall breakdown in school norms and a lack of attentiveness
to adolescents' need for challenge, structure, and personal support.
When students are bored and unchallenged, when schools do not set
and enforce high standards of behavior on a day-to-day basis, and when
schools fail to monitor behavior and then intervene to correct problems,
all the ingredients for adolescent disengagement are in place" (Roderick
et al., 1997, p. 10). Another interesting point is that while the first period
is the one most often missed, other classes throughout the day also get
skipped as can be seen in table 3.8.

Table 3.8. Missing first period does not explain truancy.

Absent 11+ Days in This Class	%
Period 1	53.0
Period 2	45.0
Period 3	42.0
Period 4	44.0
Period 5	45.0
Period 6	45.0
Period 7	48.0
Period 8	48.0
Period 9	49.0

*Second Semester, Ninth Grade, CPS 1996.

Source: Adapted from Roderick, M., Arney M., Axelman M., et al. (1997, July). Habits hard to break: A new look at truancy in Chicago's public high schools. University of Chicago. Available from http:// ccsr.uchicago.edu/publications/habits-hard-break-new-look-truancy -chicagos-public-high-schools, p. 7.

More than 50% of the ninth graders missed two or more weeks of school in their first period. However, "over 44% of the ninth graders missed two or more weeks of instruction during the middle of the day— periods 4 to 6." In addition, the findings showed that truants were just as likely to cut English as they were to cut Math (English 48%, social studies 49%, science 46%, and math 48%).

CHAPTER SUMMARY

The data found in these studies clearly suggest that truancy is much more than delinquent and disturbed students skipping school. We must include those students who truant from classes after they arrive at school in the definition of truancy.

Broadening the definition to include these students will give us a truer picture of truancy. As we broaden the definition, we will see that the majority of truancy is being done by students who are making a rational decision to skip school and class. They simply perceive that something of more value or usefulness awaits them outside the classroom.

To make meaningful steps toward a solution to this devastating problem, we must be willing to accept responsibility for this phenomenon. As we meet the truancy challenge, we can succeed in finding meaningful ways of inviting our students back to school. We can become institutions of engaged learning as opposed to drudgery and boredom.

If we embrace truancy as a school (curriculum and pedagogy) problem first and foremost, we will not only help bring our truants back to school, but we will also make our schools a more engaging and effective learning environment for *all* our students.

REFERENCES

Guare, R., & Cooper, B. S. (2003). *Truancy revisited: Students as school consumers*. Lanham, MD: Scarecrow Press, Inc.

O'Keeffe, D. (1993). *Truancy in English secondary schools: A report prepared for the DFE*. London: HMSO.

Roderick, M., Arney M., Axelman M., DaCosta K., Steiger C., Stone, S., Villarreal-Sosa, L., & Waxman, E. (1997, July). Habits hard to break: A new look at truancy in Chicago's public high schools. University of Chicago. Available from http://ccsr.uchicago.edu/publications/habits-hard-break-new-look-truancy-chicagos-public-high-schools (accessed March 2014).

Stoll, P., & O'Keeffe, D. (1989) *Officially present: An investigation into postregistration truancy in nine maintained secondary schools*. Institution of Economic Affairs. Oxford.

Chapter Four

The Ethnic Minority and English Language Learner Journey of Education

Ethnic minority and English language learner (ELL) populations in the United States have been growing dramatically over many decades, and the patterns of growth show that this increase is not going to slow down. Relatively little research has been done to identify the magnitude of the truancy problem among these growing populations.

The problem of truancy—as it relates to ethnic minorities and English language learners—stems from the same reason for truancy among Caucasians: truancy is a symptom of a much larger problem of poor teaching and poor pedagogy. We begin our study of truancy among these populations of students with a brief historical journey of their education.

Our involvement in minority education dates back 30 years to the time Dr. Shute was an undergraduate student at Brigham Young University–Hawaii Campus. During this time, he associated with many people who came mostly from the Pacific Rim countries of Asia and the Pacific Islands. Much of his association with ethnic minority students and English language learners came while he worked as a tutor in the BYU–Hawaii campus Reading Writing Center.

After graduation, Shute taught English in the Republic of Kiribati, an island nation located in the Central Pacific. Since those wonderful days in Hawaii and Kiribati, educating minority students and English language learners stimulated Shute to study the research and pedagogy associated with these populations so that he could learn how to best help.

Truancy is one key indication of how well our school system is "working" in educating our children. The high incidence and frequency levels of truancy, which will be discussed in detail in subsequent chapters of this book, indicate that these students are disappointed with the education being offered and are therefore rejecting it by truanting.

One of the greatest challenges of working with minority students is to instill in them a vision of what education could do for their quality of life. This is particularly troubling because many opportunities, programs, and resources are available for these students to receive post–high school degrees from colleges and universities, but relatively few of these students are able to see the vision and take advantage of the opportunities presented, mainly because of inadequate curricular provision and pedagogical practices in schools. Much evidence about such deficiencies is beginning to emerge.

The general evidence makes it extremely likely that the lack of motivation among many students attending schools in the United States has its roots in curricular and pedagogical inadequacies. In addition, most of the issues surrounding minority education have been politicized through education policies, programs, and legislation. This change, in turn, may have weakened the curriculum, lowered the quality of teaching, and brought confusion to even the most common terms pertaining to minority education.

Integration into the American culture and educational system by ethnic minorities was at one time a reasonably uncomplicated process. It has become more and more difficult as time has gone on, owing to the politicization of racial integration issues in recent decades. As a result, the issues required for minority students to succeed in the educational enterprise today have become more complicated.

Indeed, the politicization of integration in education has deflected the focus away from ensuring that students work hard and attend school regularly. With the loss of clarity of purpose in education, reforms require nothing more than common sense reflection to conclude that confusion must have contributed to the poor curriculum and pedagogy that have been disastrous to the more marginal or less secure of our students.

Certainly, the extensive research into truancy on which this book rests gives the strongest grounds for identifying bad curriculum, poor teaching, and weak school leadership as core variables.

THE AMERICAN MELTING POT:
AN UNCOMPLICATED ADVENTURE

At the beginning of the great American "melting pot" experience (particularly at the beginning of the 20th century), the issues surrounding race, ethnicity, and language were fairly simple. For those who immigrated to the United States came with the expectation and the desire to leave their native cultures behind to begin life anew. These immigrants spoke a variety of languages, and some did not know a word of English when they stepped ashore in the United States. The task before them was difficult to be sure.

However, when they arrived on American soil, the expectation was that they would learn English and do whatever was required to integrate fully into the dominant American culture, to become "Americans." While not easy, most immigrants met the challenge and integrated themselves into the American way, including the American educational system.

Interestingly, during this time of early immigration, the burden of responsibility for successful integration was placed squarely on the immigrant. After all, immigrants came to this country in the first place because of the dream they had of freedom, which included not only religious and political freedom but also financial security and, most importantly, educational opportunities for their children.

Parents obviously realized that they themselves were responsible for their integration. They had to measure up, as it were, to assure that they would seize the opportunities that they believed, by the grace of God, had been given them.

MINORITY EDUCATION TODAY:
FROM MERIT TO MEDIOCRITY

As time went on, the process of educational integration became intertwined with political and social issues, which made integration complicated and difficult for minority students. Later, civil rights legislation came about to assure that equal educational opportunities would be given to all minority students; but, unfortunately, as a general rule, most of them have not achieved parity with their white counterparts who make up the dominant culture.

Integration in its profound sense has not fully materialized for minority students, even though legislation was put into place that required the dominant culture to integrate them. The fact that minorities (African Americans and Hispanics in particular, as the two largest groups) have not taken full advantage of their educational opportunities is disconcerting. It is possible that, as a whole, minorities have labored under the false notion that the legislation providing equal opportunities for education was sufficient in and of itself and that their achievement would come easily.

Whatever the reason, their full integration (i.e., parity regarding academic achievement) into the dominant culture of education has been slow in coming and more and more fraught with complications and difficulties. They continue to lag behind their mainstream counterparts in academic achievement. What is even more disconcerting is that the "mainstream" students steadily and consistently decline relative to other advanced countries of the world. Also noteworthy, however, is that the learning problems of ethnic groups are not the whole puzzle. Clearly, learning English as a second (or third) language complicates educational matters for some of these pupils.

According to the *National Assessment of Educational Progress*, African Americans and Hispanic students have, on average, persistently and substantially scored below whites since the 1970s. Walberg (2001) notes, for example, that seventeen-year-old African Americans achieve at about the same level as thirteen-year-old whites, and that this divergence seems to increase as time goes on (Walberg, 2001, p. 49). Moe (2001) states in the latest *Primer on America's Schools*, arguably the best source of information about the progress of education in America, that

> mediocrity only begins to suggest the true depth of the problems that plague public education. The evidence is plain that many urban school districts [with a high preponderance of ethnic minority children] are in crisis, often failing to graduate even half of their students, and turning out graduates who in many cases can barely read, write, or do basic arithmetic. This is a crisis of quality. But it is also a crisis of social equity; the children who most desperately need educational opportunity—children who are mainly

poor and minority—are the ones trapped in our nation's worst schools. They are without hope in the absence of major reform. (Moe, 2001, pp. xv–xvi)

So far as one can see, the problems that Hispanics and African Americans face are much the same despite the language differences we have noted. They certainly seem to occupy similar niches in the achievement hierarchy, implying that what one says about the education of African Americans will usually hold for that of Hispanics.

Walter Williams, distinguished economics professor at George Mason University, and an African American, declared that "blacks themselves must solve their education problem." After reviewing the astonishingly low achievement levels among blacks, Williams says, "Teachers and politicians respond to this tragic state of affairs by saying that more money is needed" (Williams, 2006, p. A15).

He points out, however, that "the Washington, D.C. [with mostly black and minority students], school budget is about the nation's highest with about $15,000 per pupil," and "its student/teacher ratio, at 15.2 to 1, is lower than the nation's average." Despite this, Williams says that "black academic achievement in Washington, D.C., is the lowest in the nation. Reading scores for Washington's fourth-grade black students are 7 percent proficient, 21 percent basic and 71 percent below basic. For eighth graders, it's 6 percent proficient, 33 percent basic and 58 percent below basic. . . . With these achievement levels, one shouldn't be surprised that the average black high school graduate . . . has the academic achievement level of the average white sixth, seventh or eighth grader" (Williams, 2006, p. A15).

The problem cannot be attributed to racial discrimination. Williams continues, "Racial discrimination has nothing to do with what's no less than an education meltdown within the black community. Where black education is the very worst, often the city mayor is black, city council dominated by blacks, and often the school superintendent is black, as well as most of the principals and teachers . . ." Williams concludes that the "solution to black education problems is not rocket science. The problem is summoning the will" (Williams, 2006, p. A15).

Thomas Sowell (1993) is no less a proponent than Williams of this kind of thinking. His argument is interesting in that he maintains that not requiring black students to measure up sets up a "double standard," which may seem on the surface to be helping minorities but is actually hurting them. This double standard gives minority students preferential treatment with regard to admission and other advantages. Sowell argues that a double standard ultimately harms not only the educational system itself but also its intended beneficiaries.

> Academic double standards may be resented by white students but their principal victims are black students. Not even "affirmative grading" is ultimately a favor to black students, who suffer needlessly longer, until the honest grades they get convince them that they are not going to make it. Academic double standards are like certain medical procedures that do nothing to cure the disease, but simply prolong the suffering of a terminal patient. Both white and black students may end up embittered by this situation—justifiably so. (p. 294)

The number of Hispanic students is steadily increasing. "Hispanics are the fastest-growing segment of the United States population. According to the U.S. Census Bureau data, the Hispanic population increased by about 58 percent, from 22 million in 1990 to 35 million in 2000, compared with an increase of about 13 percent for the total U.S. population. In 2010, the U.S. Census Bureau estimated the number of Hispanics to be about 50.5 million, or about 16 percent of the U.S. population" (Hemphill & Vanneman, 2011, p. iii).

Much data confirm that, regrettably, these children are more likely than others to be educationally disadvantaged. "During the 1970s and 1980s, the gap between the achievement of Hispanic students and White students narrowed; however, since the 1990s, progress in the academic achievement of Hispanic students has virtually stopped" (Hansen, 2005, p. 1). For example, "Mathematics scores increased, but the achievement gap between Hispanic and White students did not change significantly at either grade 4 or 8 from 1990 to 2009. From 2007 to 2009, scores for Hispanic and White fourth graders remained unchanged" (Hemphill & Vanneman, 2011, p. iv).

Similar to mathematics, the scores increased on the reading test for both Hispanics and white students, "but the achievement gap between Hispanic and White students did not change for fourth or eighth graders when comparing 1992 to 2009. From 2007 to 2009, scores did not change significantly for either group at the fourth grade" (Hemphill& Vanneman, 2011, p. v).

In 2002 only 14% of Hispanic fourth graders scored at proficiency or advanced levels on the NAEP reading test, and "57% did not reach the 'basic' level" (Hansen, 2005, p. 1). The truth is that "at all levels, the average achievement-test scores of Hispanic students are lower than White students and by the end of high school, Hispanic students' reading and mathematical skills are comparable to those of White 13-year-olds" (Hansen, 2005, p. 1).

A wide variety of reasons is likely responsible for the low achievement of Hispanic and other minority children. "Hispanic students are more likely than white students to enter kindergarten underprepared for learning, to have to repeat a grade, to be suspended or expelled, [or] to drop out of high school (the dropout rate is twice as high as white students)" (Hansen, 2005, p. 1).

Of course, these problems contribute to truancy. Other problems that appear to "hamper [Hispanic students'] success [are]: being enrolled in less rigorous and challenging academic courses, having underprepared, less experienced teachers, [and] facing low teacher expectations . . ." (Hansen, 2005, p. 1). Truancy will likely result.

While the challenges for Hispanic students seem to be great, educators are divided on what to do to help them meet these challenges. For example, some analysts focus on the idea that minority students learn differently and require that the content and standards of subjects like mathematics be adjusted.

Peggy McIntosh, the director of the Wellesley's SEED Project on Inclusive Curriculum, claims that it is unfair and a culturally oppressive idea that the emphasis be placed on right/wrong answers (Sykes, 1996, pp. 122–23). She explains that a young girl who does not grasp the mathematic concepts involved with adding single digit numbers enters a win-lose world in which there is no way for the child to feel good about the assignment. The girl is focused on getting the answer right, but the only alternative is to get the answer wrong.

McIntosh cries out that multicultural educators need to "get beyond the win-lose world . . . with its obsession with right and wrong answers" (Sykes, 1996, p. 123). However, this kind of foolish thinking contributes to the "dumbing down" of all students, minority students included.

The reality is that we *do* live in a win-lose world, and if students cannot compute a right answer, they are destined to lose. Jamie Escalante proclaims that this shortsighted view of the abilities of ethnic minority students is one of the reasons that minority students lag so far behind others, especially whites. He states,

Our schools today . . . tend to look upon disadvantaged minority students as though they were on the verge of a mental breakdown, to be protected from any undue stress. . . . Ideas like this are not just false. They are the kiss of death for minority youth and, if allowed to proliferate, will significantly stall the advancement of minorities. (Sykes, 1996, p. 58)

Escalante and others like him have set a high standard for educating minority children. In his classes at Garfield High School in East Los Angeles, Escalante achieved astonishing success. "Instead of watering down the content of his classes or lowering his expectations, or emphasizing nebulous *mathematical communication skills*, Escalante drilled his largely Hispanic class in fundamentals of calculus . . ." (Sykes, 1996, p. 122).

Teacher expectations and a rigorous curriculum will improve Hispanic students' education opportunities. "Hispanic students need teachers who have high expectations, work with students in a supportive environment, and encourage students to succeed" (Hansen, 2005, p. 3). In addition, Hispanic student achievement can be improved "with a rigorous and challenging curriculum based on clear goals and standards. Too often Hispanic students are placed in courses with low-level curriculum and are not encouraged to enter into the more challenging courses" (Hansen, 2005, p. 3).

LANGUAGE BARRIERS

Language difficulty and the ability to adequately serve English language learners also hinder our progress. According to Padrón, Waxman, and Rivera (2002), in *Educating Hispanic Students: Obstacles and Avenues to Improved Academic Achievement*, other reasons for the low achievement of Hispanic students include the lack of qualified teachers and the use of inappropriate teaching practices.

As for the lack of qualified teachers, they explain that the number of teachers who are qualified ESL (English as a second language) or bilingual teachers is woefully low. These unqualified teachers are expected to teach content to many Hispanic students who are learning English as a second language.

In fact, 37% of Hispanic students in grade 4 and 21% of Hispanic students in grade 8 are English language learners (Hemphill & Vanneman, 2011, p.

iii). In concentrated areas where ELLs attend school, ". . . over 84% of the 54 largest urban school districts reported that they had non-credentialed teachers on their staff" (Padrón, Waxman, & Rivera, 2002, p. 9).

Most of these teachers of ELL students said they felt unprepared to meet the needs of their students, and in a recent national survey of classroom teachers "57% of all teachers responded that they either very much needed or somewhat needed more information on helping students with limited English proficiency achieve to high standards" (Padrón, Waxman, Rivera, 2002, p. 9).

In other words, teachers who teach English language learners should possess knowledge and training on how students learn a second language. Even though the minority students are being taught in English, this knowledge and training will help teachers fashion lessons and activities in such a way as to assure understanding of the content by the minority students, thus helping them achieve high standards.

Sykes (1996) maintains that while "white educationists continue to devise elaborate 'multicultural' curricula for inner-city public schools . . ., a handful of innovative schools are drawing attention precisely for their rigorous programs and traditionalist approach to learning" (p. 286).

Sykes favors the approach that E. D. Hirsch propounds, which does not condescend minority students. "What is striking about Hirsch's curriculum is its lack of condescension; it makes no concessions to allegedly different styles of learning or the arguments that poor, minority students need to be given a less challenging course of study" (1996, p. 286).

These voices, and others, come from minds that can see through the fog of educational double talk and the politicization of education. They focus on the fact that hard work and persistent study are the essential ingredients if *anyone* is to become an educated person. The point, though, is that the innovative schools in question are doing their part of the job properly; they are teaching minorities as if the fact of their minority status had no bearing on their achievement. And, indeed, it has not.

DISTRACTING ISSUES

Literally millions of words have been written on the subject of minority and racial integration and education, but most of them have simply distracted us from the real issue. For example, Signithia Fordham maintains that a "terrible price must be paid to enter the dominant cultural world" (Shapiro & Purpel, 1995, p.134). Access, for example, to the "American dream" requires a renunciation of one's allegiance to a native culture and community.

Fordham claims that "schools communicate the message that black adolescents cannot be culturally different and achieve success as defined by the dominant society." She further claims that "ultimately, black Americans must question whether they are willing to 'sublimate' individual goals in favor of a commitment to the integrity of the existing cultural system and 'the collective advancement of our people'" (Shapiro & Purpel, 1993, p. 134).

The anthropologist John Ogbu says that the problem lies in the "forced immigration and slavery of African American ancestors" (Walberg, 2001, p. 49). This kind of statement is posturing sentimentality. We might ask: why should the descendants of poor Chinese and Japanese immigrants, who faced huge discrimination when they arrived in America, do so well at school and college? Why should the Jews, who always face some degree of prejudice, do so well in academic life?

Expressions like those of Fordham and Ogbu tend to obscure, not clarify, the problems that create the gap existing between the achievement of minority students and the achievement of white students.

Other scholars claim that the problem lies in the "historically deficient education systems" in the South and "inferior schools for rural blacks in southern states" (Walberg, 2001, p. 49). They suggest that blacks still have not recovered from these deficiencies even generations after migrating to big industrial cities in the North. Again, this is unconvincing. Why do Asian children so often succeed in our schools?

Some scholars belonging to ethnic minorities reject, as we have seen, unnecessary excuses. Another explanation for the achievement gap, from those who reject such excuses, is the "victim" mentality, which some people use as an excuse for mediocrity. If we encourage self-pity and mediocrity, they are likely to perpetuate themselves.

John McWhorter (2001), in *Losing the Race: Self-Sabotage in Black America*, says that in his view "as a black faculty observer at the university, a cult of victimology transforms a problem to be solved into a persistent black identity of anti-intellectualism, separatism, and cultural disconnect from learning." (p. 7)

Charles Sykes, in his well-known book *A Nation of Victims*, essentially says the same thing, that "victimism has co-opted the genuine victories of the civil rights movement for less worthy goals" (Sykes, 1992, p. fly leaf).

Another negative side effect that ethnic minority students and English language learners face is a result of constant voices they hear from the so-called crusaders for minority civil rights: "stereotype vulnerability." This phenomenon occurs

> when victims of negative stereotypes face a task that popular prejudice says they are not very good at but that they nonetheless want to do and believe they can do, they cannot escape the shadow of the beliefs around them. . . . The more they care about doing well in that domain, the more such a thought bothers them. At minimum, it distracts them; at worst, it prods them to prove the popular prejudice wrong. Either way, their awareness of the negative stereotype adds a level of anxiety that others do not face, and the resulting stress slows and harms performance, which in turn produces even more anguish, causing additional reminders, and so forth. (Bain, 2004, p. 69)

In other words, the loud voices that continually preach that ethnic minorities are victims without civil rights put undue psychological (perhaps subconscious) pressure on ethnic minority students. "People who face repeated messages that they are inferior in a certain kind of activity (schoolwork, for example) will often decide to drop out and build a life in another area" (Bain, 2004, p. 68). Therefore, the life of mediocrity, poverty, and other social problems that ethnic minorities face becomes a self-fulfilling prophecy, which leaders of those communities continue to perpetuate.

THE DISTRACTION OF LANGUAGE INSTRUCTION

A natural byproduct of ethnic diversity in our schools is language difference. The magnitude of this issue is illustrated by, "According to the U.S. Department of Education, more than 5 million ELLs were enrolled in public schools in 2003, about 1 in every 10 students, and these students brought with them more than 425 first languages" (Flannery, 2006, p. 25). In California alone, 12,401,756 (39.5%) people speak a language other than English (mostly Spanish). And 31.0% of the people who speak Spanish speak English "not well" or "not at all" (U.S. Census Bureau website).

Researchers point out that an obvious lack of English skills alone cannot account for the low academic achievement of English language learners, and that speaking a language other than English, of course, is not a handicap in and of itself. In fact, bilingualism can be a great asset, and many people who speak English as a second language have succeeded and continue to succeed in school and society.

Some argue that what *is* important, however, is the way schools and teachers perceive these language differences and whether modifications in the curriculum can be made. Hence, the seemingly endless controversy over programs and classifications continues.

"Bilingual education" is the term used in the American education system to describe the services provided for these children who speak English as a second language. Bilingual programs are those in which instruction of the student involves the use of two languages: English and the child's first language. Usually, the child receives content area instruction in the native language while at the same time learning English as a second language.

However, "only about 15 percent of students needing special language services are in federally funded bilingual programs; only about one-third are receiving any language assistance at all. In addition, the percentage of students in bilingual programs has actually declined in some places since 1980" (Shapiro & Purpel, 1995, p. 197). Bilingual programs, in theory, should also incorporate cultural aspects from both languages, emphasizing the students' history, traditions, and native culture.

ESL instruction differs from bilingual instruction primarily because the students' native language is not used during instruction. ESL focuses on teaching English language skills with the goal that the student can, at some point, understand content area instruction in English. An obvious problem is that while ESL students struggle with English, they simultaneously struggle in the content area courses because the courses are being taught in English.

Like other educational issues involving ethnic minorities, controversies with bilingual ESL students have arisen over the years. Whether to mandate bilingual programs, the naming of programs, the extent of the bilingual instruction in the program, and what constitutes a successful program are some controversial issues.

One cannot help contrasting the former American policy of ignoring the Italian, Hungarian, Polish, Yiddish, and other languages, which children spoke at home, with the present concern with their home language. It is not obvious that the present posture is an improvement over the earlier one.

Early on in United States history (and this is also true today), people felt the effects of the huge migration of people into our country. Patriotic unity was continually emphasized, in some cases being directly tied to concerns with speaking the English language. Related to an English language policy, President Theodore Roosevelt said, "We have room for but one language here, and that is the English language; for we intend to see that the crucible turns our people out as Americans, of American nationality, and not as dwellers in a polyglot boardinghouse" (Shapiro & Purpel, 1995, p. 200).

Do not Roosevelt's words here show the truth that convincing sentiment and vivid language often go together? These words make a vivid contrast with the sort of dead prose favored by multiculturalism. President Roosevelt's pronouncement started a movement toward an "Englishonly" policy in the United States. This push lasted many years.

Then the ideological climate changed. In 1971 Massachusetts became the first state to mandate bilingual education programs (Shapiro & Purpel, 1995, p. 198). Next, in 1974 the U.S. Supreme Court ruled unanimously in the *Lau v. Nichols* case that students who did not understand the language of instruction were having their civil rights violated. The court stated,

> There is no equality of treatment merely by providing students with the same facilities, textbooks, teachers, and curriculum; for students who do not understand English are effectively foreclosed from any meaningful education. Basic skills are at the very core of what these public schools teach. Imposition of a requirement that, before a child can effectively participate in the educational program, he must already have acquired those basic skills is to make a mockery of public education. (Shapiro & Purpel, 1995, p. 203)

What constitutes a person's civil rights is an important question. Legislation that enables that person to coast through education with low achievement and mediocrity is a muddled response to that question and is becoming more and more muddled as the years pass. Adversaries of bilingual education believe that it is not in the child's best interest to allow such concessions as they only prolong these students' need to learn English. Proponents of bilingual education believe that without it, "millions of children are doomed to educational underachievement" and failure (Shapiro & Purpel, 1995, p. 203).

But President Roosevelt was not the only president who felt strongly about this issue. President Ronald Reagan said the following in response to a question about support for bilingual education: "It is absolutely wrong and against American concept to have a bilingual education program that is now openly, admittedly dedicated to preserving their native language and never getting them adequate in English so they can go out into the job market" (Shapiro & Purpel, 1995, p. 200).

In short, language differences in and of themselves cannot be seen as barriers to learning, but a history of the language policies in our society has resulted in making them so. "Language policies and practices in the United States have ranged from grudging acceptance of language diversity to outright hostility" (Shapiro & Purpel, 1995, pp. 207–8).

This myriad of policies, practices, and classifications has led to complicating the matter and diluting our curriculum. Truth be told, we are a nation that welcomes its immigrants. And while they are expected to work hard, they must be given the proper tools to be successful, which include an appropriate curriculum and proper pedagogy.

RACE AND ETHNICITY:
FALSE DISTINCTIONS OR ESSENTIAL ONES?

We now turn to a discussion of the terms used to distinguish the various ethnic or racial backgrounds. Many problems are associated with the terms "race" and "ethnicity," but certain conventional categories of differentiation are necessary for purposes of empirical research in education.

In a perfect world, the divisions among human beings would be neat and manageable, and the terms referring to them would be clear and convenient for a researcher in the social sciences to use. However, in our world, an untidy and in some ways unmanageable complexity exists.

The terms Caucasian, African American, Hispanic, and Asian are highly problematic as precise definitions. Nevertheless, while they *are* problematic, these terms are commonly used and understood in the United States for the general categorization of ethnic backgrounds.

If one is to investigate any research topic in education, these terms are imposed by research conventions. Therefore it seems useful to clarify briefly the terms that are used to categorize the various ethnic groups.

However, the terms we use in identifying these various categories of ethnic minorities are, let us repeat, fraught with difficulty. For example, Thomas Sowell has said, speaking of the broad classification of the word *minority*, that

> the massive ethnic communities that make up the mosaic of American society cannot be adequately described as "minorities." There is no "majority." The largest single identifiable ethnic strain is people of British ancestry—who make up just 15 percent of the American population. They barely outnumber German Americans (13 percent) or blacks (11 percent). Millions of Americans cannot identify themselves at all ethnically, due to intermixtures over the generations. (Sowell, 1981, p. 4)

So the terms themselves—Caucasian, African American, Native American, Hispanic, and Asian—ultimately have no precise definition. Even notions of "race" and "ethnicity" are notoriously problematic and unstable. The words "race" and "ethnicity" are now used largely synonymously, although "ethnicity" is becoming the more common term in research. "Race" originally meant the genetic differentiation of the world's population in terms of skin color, skull shape, and other physical features. However, widespread agreement today is that no "pure" races exist and that all so-called races are in reality racially mixed.

The term "ethnicity" has arisen as a modification of "race" perhaps because of the perceived shortcomings of the latter. Human racial groups are thought to be modified by cultural and historical circumstances, especially language. The result is the translation of "race" into "ethnicity." Over time, the two separate terms have drifted back into something close to synonymous meanings. For the most part, the terms are used interchangeably. However, we should remember the unsatisfactory nature of both terms if we intend to make *fine* distinctions.

Whether we are thinking of race or ethnicity, terms like Caucasian, African American, or Hispanic are virtually useless for delicate or precise discussion, but they are not entirely useless. It does mean that their use demands care. They are all problematic and certainly conceal as much or more than they reveal. In other words, on top of the complex mixture of races lies the even more complex nature of culture and languages.

For practical purposes in most aspects of society, be it the medical world, the education system, or government censuses, at times the need arises to classify, in more detail than the word "citizen" gives us, these many peoples who now call America their home.

Perhaps one of the most widely agreed upon categorizations for ethnic groups in America is the United States census. The United States has, since the 1960s, used data on race and ethnicity extensively for the purposes of civil rights monitoring, employment, voting rights, housing and mortgage lending, health care services, and educational opportunities (Office of Management and Budget, 1995, p. 3).

Collecting data on race, one can imagine, has been a complex undertaking by the federal government, and the process has come under some criticism. Should the federal government collect data on race and ethnicity? Those who favor no collection of data on race and ethnicity claim that collecting race information is divisive, archaic, and unscientific. They feel that race information does not need to be known by the federal government, and that the categories are meaningless since everyone is a mixture with no pure races.

In addition, everyone is supposed to have equal protection under the law, so race does not matter. Finally, categorizing race is dehumanizing (Office of Management and Budget, 1995, p. 7).

Others think that the collection of such data is essential. However, exactly what the specific data collection and presentation categories should be are confusing, without clear, unambiguous, objective, generally agreed-upon definitions of the terms "race" and "ethnicity." The controversy over categorization has been discussed at great length, and one becomes dizzy trying to wade through all the references. Race can be categorized according to religion, ancestry, culture, or many other areas.

The current broad categories of race in America are white, black, Asian or Pacific Islander, American Indian or Alaskan Native, and Hispanic origin (Office of Management and Budget, 1995, p. 15). The white category "includes persons having origins in any of the original peoples of Europe, North Africa, or the Middle East" (Office of Management and Budget, 1995, p. 15).

A geographically oriented subcategory has been suggested for people with "Middle Eastern" origins. In addition, "Caucasian" and "Anglo" are alternative words suggested to describe the white category (Office of Management and Budget, 1995, p. 17). Caucasian groups involve an immensely complex racial and ethnic mosaic. Anglo-Saxon, Slavic, Germanic, Celtic, Greek, Jews, and many more are all termed Caucasian.

The term "black" refers to people having origins in any of the black racial groups of Africa. African American and black African American have been suggested as alternate names for blacks. In addition, there have been suggestions to create a separate category for Creoles and blacks born in Brazil or the Caribbean, as these people do not identify with the term "African American" (Office of Management and Budget, 1995, p. 20).

For purposes of a study on truancy, categories are needed that are commonly used among the students so that the students can accurately identify their ethnicity. Common documents identify the terms used to classify ethnic background.

On the United States 2000 Census form, questions 7 and 8 refer to race/ethnicity. Respondents to the census are asked to answer both questions. The basic differences between the 2000 census and the 1990 census as pertaining to ethnic categories were (1) the Pacific Islanders are separated from Asians and (2) respondents are allowed to mark more than one race (Washington State Office of Financial Management, March 2001).

We may ask ourselves why the census in question 8 separates Filipinos from Asian or Pacific Islanders yet does not differentiate between Creoles or blacks from Brazil from the black/African American/Negro category.

It is also interesting to note that question 7 asks everyone (whites, blacks, Asians, etc.) if they are Hispanic/Latino. This seems to show that the United States is now a country where its citizens are identified first and foremost by whether or not they are Hispanic. "If you are not Hispanic, then what are you? White? Black? Asian?, etc."

For the 2000 census data, the basic categories are Hispanic/Latino, white, black/African American, American Indian, or Alaskan Native. The categories for Asians and Pacific Islanders were more distinct.

In addition, all parents wishing to enroll their children in public school must fill out a form that asks them their ethnic background. A typical school enrollment form will ask for race/ethnic origin (Caucasian/white, black/African American, Hispanic, Asian, Pacific Islander, and Native American). Parents and guardians are also asked their language preference, usually requesting for language most often spoken at home.

It is not uncommon for the forms to ask for further language information, specifically languages spoken by the mother, father, family members, and the language the student speaks most often.

While all ethnic backgrounds are complex, the terms we can logically use for most research purposes are Caucasian/white, black/African American, Hispanic, Native American, Asian, and Pacific Islander. It would be difficult to ask the children if they are Italian, Irish, Polish, Hungarian, English, Finnish, Greek, Jews, Norwegian, and so on.

All these groups are interpenetrated. In many cases, the students would not know the details of their ancestry. We cannot ask African Americans how "African" they are. How would they know? We cannot ask Hispanics how "Spanish" they are or Native Americans how "Native American" they are. In other words, we cannot use "micro" categories because they are usually not available. Whether we like it or not, we have to use "macro" categories. And while these macro categories may indeed hide more than they reveal, this does not mean that they reveal nothing.

In the next chapter of this book, we present data from a major truancy study in the western United States. Our racial/ethnic data in no sense explain the differential tendency to truant between these groups. But we have no basis for rejecting the data on their truancy simply because the categories are in various respects unsatisfactory. We must accept that these ethnic distinctions cannot be investigated other than in their highly aggregated form, the one understood and used commonly by people in the United States.

CHAPTER SUMMARY

The issues surrounding race and ethnicity have become extremely complicated over the past 100 years. In the early part of the 20th century, masses of people came to American shores. And whereas at that time the issues were relatively simple and uncomplicated regarding integration into the educational culture, over time they have become more and more complicated. For example, the politicizing of our schools has left us with a cluttered, poor curriculum and mediocre teaching. Massive numbers of students have been exiting this system in the form of truancy.

Be that as it may, voices have emerged from the African American, Hispanic, and other minority communities who seemingly are able to see through the unnecessary complications and are demanding that they assume responsibility for the education of their children, much as was required in early America, at least in the early part of the 20th century.

Many of these thoughtful voices believe that they must make the changes that would bring about better achievement on the part of their children. Those changes—including regular attendance at school—must occur in the schools as well as in students, parents, and political leaders.

All the while, the issues have become more and more complicated, affecting greatly the very language researchers use to study minority education. The classification of terms is so controversial that individual researchers must make decisions about definitions and categories themselves and exert every effort to defend those decisions.

Documents and forms currently in use in government, youth organizations, and schools help us to understand the terms people commonly use to identify their racial background. While these terms are not technically fully viable, they are all we have.

If the basic subjects of the curriculum (e.g., English and mathematics) are poorly taught, the effects may be disproportionately adverse on the performance of ethnic minority students. For example, African Americans may come from poorer homes with less material and intellectual resources than the average and may find unsatisfactory teaching of these basic subjects very hard to cope with and build upon.

And to further complicate matters, the subjects that presume a solid background in English or math, such as history and science, will assuredly prove difficult. This effect, however, is not obviously different from what we would expect from white working-class children of similar low-income backgrounds.

The children of African American parents may have had their education impaired by all the attention given to the racial equality movement in all its historical complexity. This is not to question the soundness of racial equality as a moral and political objective; rather it is to raise the possibility that the attention given to it has gone beyond reasonable limits.

Some writers have alleged that all the emphasis on race may be counterproductive and may actually suppress student performance. These racial issues are often quite explosive, but they surely must be considered in any study pertaining to truancy.

Another problem for those who claim that racist attitudes are at the root of poor performance of African American students is that other ethnic minorities' performance is as good or better than average, even when English is *not* the language of choice spoken at home. In other words, the absence of English in the home may be an extra difficulty, one that some ethnic minority students appear to have dealt with quite successfully.

To compound matters further, for the students with lower material resources, and in whose homes English is not spoken, a demand may be that they work many nights a week; yet despite all this, they may have low truancy levels. Minority students also battle ethnic, linguistic, cultural, and racial difficulties.

When we confront the data accumulated during the course of this research, we will see that although a huge truancy problem exists in many American schools, the patterns are not always neatly packaged and often cannot be explained simply or mechanistically.

The question of differing behavior of ethnic groups has fascinated sociologists and other social scientists for many years. Many nations have become increasingly ethnically diverse over the last 30 years. Thus far, then, no straightforward explanations exist for the ethnic variations in truancy patterns.

This leads us to raise a number of questions: Are the students of different ethnic backgrounds (Caucasian, African American, Hispanic, Asian) distinctly patterned in their truancy? Do variables such as age, sex, language spoken at home, extracurricular activities at school, grade point average, having guardians as opposed to parents, belonging to one-parent families rather than two-parent families, days/hours of work, bedtime, and length of time living at current address make a difference?

For the immigrant truants, the family may own a business that will not survive if the young family members do not spend some of their days working. Immigrants are known for their hard work ethic as their days and nights are spent at the family business. A school-aged child's help may be desperately needed. This suggests that in order to cope with an immediate crisis, the parents give up long-term opportunity and success for their children.

With the historically high levels of immigration into the United States, we find ourselves at a crossroads. Should we continue to try to locate the causes of truancy in the deficiencies of the foreigner, just as in the past we have located them in the shortcomings of American students? Or could we look closer at the possibility of the institution also being at fault?

REFERENCES

Bain, K. (2004). *What the best college teachers do.* Cambridge, MA: Harvard University Press.

Flannery, M. E. (2006, January). Language can't be a barrier. *NEA Today*, p. 25.

Hansen, A. L. (2005). *Hispanic student achievement.* Research brief. The Principal's Partnership. www.principalspartnership.com.

Hemphill, F. C., & Vanneman, A. (2011). *Achievement gaps: How Hispanic and white students in public schools perform in mathematics and reading on the national assessment of educational progress (NCES 2011-459).* National Center for Education Statistics, Institute of Education Sciences, U.S. Department of Education. Washington, D.C.

McWhorter, J. H. (2001). *Losing the race: Self-sabotage in black America.* New York: Simon & Schuster.

Moe, T. M. (Ed.). (2001). *A primer on America's schools.* Stanford, CA: Hoover Institution Press.

Office of Management and Budget. (1995, August). Standards for the classification of federal data on race and ethnicity. http://www.whitehouse.gov/omb/fedreg_race-ethnicity (retrieved March 4, 2014).

Padrón, Y. N., Waxman, H. C., & Rivera, H. H. (2002). *Educating Hispanic students: Obstacles and avenues to improved academic achievement.* Center for Research on Education, Diversity & Excellence, University of California.

Shapiro, H. S., & Purpel, D. E. (Eds.) (1995). *Critical social issues in American education: Toward the twenty-first century.* New York: Longman.

Sowell, T. (1981). *Ethnic America: A history.* New York: Basic Books, Inc.

Sowell, T. (1993). *Inside American education: The decline, the deception, the dogmas.* New York: The Free Press.

Sykes, C. J. (1992). *A nation of victims: The decay of the American character.* New York: St. Martin's Press.

Sykes, C. J. (1996). *Dumbing down our kids: Why American children feel good about themselves but can't read, write, or add.* New York: St. Martin's Griffin.

U.S. Census Bureau. http://factfinder2.census.gov (retrieved March 4, 2014).

Walberg, H. J. (2001). Achievement in American schools. In T. Moe (Ed.), *A primer on America's schools.* Stanford, CA: Hoover Institution Press.

Washington State Office of Financial Management. (March 2001). *Understanding Census 2000: Race category changes & comparisons. Population estimates & projections.* Research Brief No. 12.

Williams, W. (2006, July 5). Blacks themselves must solve their education problem. *Deseret Morning News*, p. A15.

Chapter Five

Truancy and Ethnicity

As highlighted in the previous chapter, the ethnic minority and English language learner populations continue to grow at a staggering rate in the United States. America has always been a nation where cultural and ethnic diversity has flourished. This diversity, of course, presents national challenges and specific challenges in education.

As we have seen, one of these challenges is truancy. The main purpose of this chapter is to explore the truancy problem as it relates to the ethnic minority students.

Very little research has been done with regard to asking truants why they truant, and even less research has focused on ethnic minority truant behavior. A major research project was conducted in the western United States to ask students why they truant (Shute, 2009). The research instrument elicited data to determine the ethnicity of the participants. These data were then used to explore truancy in relation to ethnicity.

The research survey was administered to 692 ethnic minority students and found that 71.4% of the students admitted to being truant during the two months prior to taking the survey. The details of this study will be outlined in the following discussion, first with truancy by ethnicity and gender, then type of truancy, and, finally, frequency of truancy. This chapter also discusses in depth the phenomenon of near truancy behavior and the findings we discovered.

OVERALL TRUANCY BY ETHNICITY AND GENDER

One important goal of this research was to determine truancy factors pertaining to race and gender. In other words, do girls or boys of the ethnic groups participating in this study have a higher incidence of truancy? Seven main ethnic groups were represented in this study, each with a fairly even distribution of boys and girls.

Table 5.1 shows the incidence of truancy by ethnicity of the participants and their gender. The information in the table starts with two main categories: Caucasians and ethnic minorities. The data for the main ethnic minority group do not include figures from the "other" category for reasons that will be explained later. Under these main groupings are the data for the specific ethnic groups that participated in this research. These data are sorted by largest ethnic population except for the "other" group.

As noted earlier, the participants were asked to identify their ethnicity. Seven races were listed (Caucasian, Hispanic, Asian, Pacific Islander, African American, Native American, Middle East) as well as an "other" category. Interestingly, 101 students classified themselves as "other." After perusing over 1,100 of the questionnaires to identify the nature of responses to the "other" category, a brief explanation is required.

Of the 1,100 surveys, 43 had "other" checked. To begin with, 13 of these responses were left blank (the student simply checked the box marked "other" without specifying a race). Nine students specified "white" (one of them wrote "wite"), 4 specified "American," 2 listed "Irish," and 5 listed "Greek." The following received 1 each: Spanish, Middle East, Asian American, Canadian, Hawaiian, Brown, and white/ Polynesian. All of these, of course, should have been classified in a different existing choice on the survey. Two legitimate responses were discovered. One was from a student who listed "Aborigine" and one was from a student who listed "East Indian." And, for icing on the cake, one student simply put "why do you care?" (question mark added by researcher).

In the tables that follow, the data that correspond with the "other" category are not included with the ethnic minority group category. Furthermore, we will analyze the data in relation to two general ethnicities: Caucasian and ethnic minorities.

Table 5.1 shows the ethnicity and gender of the participants. Overall, Caucasians made up the highest percentage of participants in the study

Table 5.1. **Truancy by race and gender (incidence of truancy).**

	Total Boys (%)	Boy Truants (%)	Total Girls (%)	Girl Truants (%)
Caucasians	941	598	993	606
	(48.7)	(63.5)	(51.3)	(61.0)
Minority Groups*	345	257	347	237
	(49.9)	(74.5)	(50.1)	(68.3)
Hispanic	181	146	180	133
	(50.1)	(80.7)	(49.9)	(73.9)
African American	27	20	29	21
	(48.2)	(74.1)	(51.8)	(72.4)
Asian	67	39	65	37
	(50.8)	(58.2)	(49.2)	(56.9)
Native American	19	15	23	16
	(45.2)	(78.9)	(54.8)	(69.6)
Pacific Islander	46	34	42	25
	(52.3)	(73.9)	(47.7)	(59.5)
Middle East	5	3	8	5
	(38.5)	(60.0)	(61.5)	(62.5)
Other	57	39	44	26
	(56.4)	(68.4)	(43.6)	(59.1)

* Does not include the "other" category.

followed by Hispanics. The percentage of boys and girls in the study were similar.

Obviously, some of the ethnic groups did not have enough participants to provide statistically valid data. However, a total of 692 ethnic minority students completed the survey, and the results provide incredibly useful and valid data. Of the 2,727 students who took the survey, 1,934 (70.9%) claimed to be Caucasian. This represents the largest ethnic group. Of these 1,934 Caucasian students, 941 (48.7%) were boys and 993 (51.3%) were girls.

A total of 692 (25.4%) students claimed to be one of the ethnic minority groups, not including the students in the "other" category, though inevitably some of these students were minorities. Of these 692 ethnic minority students, 345 (49.9%) were boys and 347 (50.1%) were girls.

The similar percentages between the ethnic minority boys and the Caucasian boys are interesting, and the similarity in the percentages between the ethnic minority girls and Caucasian girls is remarkable. One will notice in table 5.1 the even distribution of boys and girls among the different ethnic groups represented in this study.

Overall, of the 941 Caucasian boys, 598 (63.5%) said they had truanted in the two months prior to taking the survey. Of the 993 Caucasian girls, 606 (61.0%) truanted. This shows a nearly even percentage of Caucasian boys and girls who were truant. Of the 345 ethnic minority boys, 257 (74.5%) truanted, and of the 347 ethnic minority girls, 237 (68.3%) truanted. This shows that more ethnic minority boys than ethnic minority girls truanted, although the difference is 6.3%. As a whole, a higher percentage of ethnic minority boys truanted than Caucasian boys, and a higher percentage of ethnic minority girls truanted than Caucasian girls.

A breakdown of the specific ethnic minority truancy levels shows that Hispanic boys truant most. Of the 181 Hispanic boys, 146 (80.7%) were truants. Hispanic girls also had the highest level of truancy out of the ethnic minority girls. Of the 180 Hispanic girls, 133 (73.9%) were truants. Asian students showed the lowest percentage of truanting. Of the 67 Asian boys, 39 (58.2%) truanted, and of the 65 Asian girls, 37 (56.9%) truanted.

The widest difference in truancy levels came from the Pacific Islander boys and girls. Of the 46 Pacific Islander boys, 34 (73.9%) truanted, and of the 42 Pacific Islander girls, 25 (59.5%) truanted—a difference of 14.4%.

While clearly the boys had higher levels of truancy than the girls in all the ethnic groups except one (Middle East), we see shockingly high levels of truancy among all ethnic groups of boys and girls. Traditional views of truancy claim that boys have a higher incidence of truancy than girls. Other research opposes this claim. To examine this question in a bit more detail, the data were analyzed using a t-test. Table 5.2 shows the results.

The data show that 74.5% (SD .44) of the ethnic boys truanted while 68.3% (SD .47) of the ethnic girls truanted. The t-statistic was 1.80 that was significant above the <.05 level of confidence (p = .0358). This analysis shows that the incidence of truancy among ethnic boys is significantly higher than that of ethnic girls.

But the same was not true for the Caucasian truants. The data show that 63.5% (SD .48) of the Caucasian boys truanted, and 61.0% (SD .49) of the Caucasian girls truanted. While a greater percentage of the Caucasian boys truanted, the t-test (1.14, p = .1264) showed the difference was not statistically significant.

Therefore, the traditional view that boys are more likely to have a higher incidence of truancy is statistically verified for these ethnic minority students as a group, but it is not statistically supported for Caucasian students.

Table 5.2. Simple statistics for truancy among male and female Caucasian and ethnic students.

Group	n	# Truants	Truancy Level	SD
Ethnic Girls	347	237	68.3%	0.47
Ethnic Boys	345	257	74.5%	0.44
Caucasian Girls	993	606	61.0%	0.49
Caucasian Boys	941	598	63.5%	0.48

T-test for comparing hypothesis that ethnic boys are *more* likely to truant than ethnic girls, and Caucasian boys are *more* likely to truant than Caucasian girls.

Test for Ethnic and Caucasian Boy and Girl Truants	T-Stat	P-Value
Ethnic boys greater than ethnic girls	1.80	.0358*
Caucasian boys greater than Caucasian girls	1.14	.1264

* Indicates significance at or beyond <0.05.

In general, truancy existed in large proportions among all the ethnic groups that participated in this study. Table 5.3 shows the results of the survey and compares the truancy behavior of Caucasian students and ethnic minority students according to the type of truancy in which these students engaged. Students were asked if they truanted from (1) only entire days of school, (2) only certain classes after arriving at school, or (3) both entire days of school and one or more classes after arriving at school. Students indicated only one type of truancy in which they engaged.

These data support the findings of other truancy studies, namely that of O'Keeffe (1993) in the United Kingdom and Guare and Cooper (2003) in New York, in that the majority of truancy is class truancy, meaning those students who arrive at school and truant from one or more classes throughout the day. The incidence of class truancy is more than double that of school truancy.

Specifically, of the 494 ethnic minority truants, 105 (21.3%) engaged in school truancy, 225 (45.5%) engaged in class truancy, and 164 (33.2%)

Table 5.3. Truancy by ethnicity and type.

	Total (%)	Nontruants (%)	Total Truants (%)	School Truants (%)	Class Truants (%)	Both (%)
Caucasians	1,934	730	1,204	211	616	377
	(100)	(37.7)	(62.3)	(17.5)	(51.2)	(31.3)
Minority Groups*	692	198	494	105	225	164
	(25.4)	(28.6)	(71.4)	(21.3)	(45.5)	(33.2)

* Does not include the "other" category.

truanted from both entire days of school and from one or more classes. Class truancy is the favorite among the ethnic minority groups, although by not as large a margin as in the case of the Caucasian truants.

In addition to itemizing the types of truancy, these data show that the incidence of truancy among ethnic minority students (71.4%) is higher than that among Caucasian students (62.3%). We know truancy levels are high among students in general but highest among ethnic minority students.

Table 5.4 provides statistics for truancy among ethnic minorities and Caucasian students as measured by race and shows the truancy levels of Caucasian students to the Hispanic, Asian, African American, and Pacific Islander students.

First, the study compared Caucasian students with the other major ethnic groups. The level of truancy for Caucasians was 62.3% (SD .48), while the incidence of truancy for all other ethnic groups combined was 71.4% (SD .45). This difference was highly significant beyond the <.05 level (p < .0000). Thus the data show that in general ethnic minority students have a higher incidence of truancy (t = −4.47).

When the data from the various ethnic groups were analyzed separately against the Caucasian group, the t-tests showed that both the differences

Table 5.4. Simple statistics for truancy among ethnic and Caucasian students.

Group	n	# Truants	Truancy Level	SD
Caucasian	1,934	1,204	62.3%	0.48
Ethnic	692	494	71.4%	0.45
Hispanic	361	279	77.3%	0.42
Asian	132	76	57.6%	0.50
African American	56	41	73.2%	0.45
Pacific Islander	88	59	67.0%	0.47

T-test for comparing hypothesis that ethnic students are *more* likely to truant than Caucasian students.

Test for Ethnic and Caucasian Students	T-Stat	P-Value
Ethnic truancy greater than Caucasian truancy	−4.47	.0000*
Hispanic truancy greater than Caucasian truancy	−6.09	.0000*
Asian truancy greater than Caucasian truancy	1.05	.1470
African American truancy greater than Caucasian truancy	−1.80	.0356*
Pacific Islander truancy greater than Caucasian truancy	−093 −0.93	.1766

* Indicates significance at or beyond <0.05.

in truancy incidence levels between Hispanics (77.3%, SD .42) and Caucasians (62.3%, SD .48, t = –6.09, p < .0000) and between African Americans (73.2%, SD .45) and Caucasians (62.3%, SD .48) (t = –1.80, p = .0356) also were significant.

However, the incidence of truancy for the Asian and Pacific Islander groups, when compared to the Caucasian group, was not significant. Interestingly, the incidence of truancy among the Asian students (57.6%, SD .50) in the study (N=132) was not only lower than that of all other ethnic groups but also below that of the Caucasian group.

FREQUENCY OF TRUANCY

This study also gathered data regarding how often the students truanted. The participants responded to the question "Which of the following best describes how often you cut school or class in the last 2 months?" The students were asked to check only *one* of three options. The first option given was "not very often (e.g., 1–2 *days* or 1-2 *classes*)." The second option was "often (e.g., 1 *day* a week or 1–2 *classes* a week)." The third option was "very often (e.g., 2 or more *days* a week or 2 or more *classes* a week)." Table 5.5 shows how the students responded to this item on the survey.

Without exception, most truancy takes place "not very often." Overall, of the 1,204 Caucasian truants, 944 (78.4%) said they do not truant very often—only 1–2 days or classes in the two months prior to taking the survey. Another 172 (14.3%) said they had truanted 1 day or class per week, and 88 (7.3%) said they had truanted 2 or more days or classes per week.

Comparatively, of the 494 minority truants, 353 (71.5%) also said they had truanted not very often—only 1–2 days or classes in the two months prior to taking the survey. Another 93 respondents (18.8%) said they had truanted 1 day or class a week, and 48 truants (9.7%) said they had truanted 2 or more days a week during the previous two months. The ethnic minority students admitted to a higher frequency of truancy than the Caucasian students in each category. The Asian students were the only group who truanted with less frequency than the Caucasian students in the "very often" category.

Table 5.5.   Frequency of truancy.

	Not Very Often 1–2 Days/Classes (%)	Often 1 Day/Class a Week (%)	Very Often 2+ Days/ Classes Week (%)	Total Truants
Caucasians	944 (78.4)	172 (14.3)	88 (7.3)	1204
Minority Groups*	353 (71.5)	93 (18.8)	48 (9.7)	494
Hispanic	202 (72.4)	49 (17.6)	28 (10.0)	279
African American	21 (51.2)	11 (26.8)	9 (22.0)	41
Asian	62 (81.6)	13 (17.1)	1 (1.3)	76
Native American	21 (67.7)	6 (19.4)	4 (12.9)	31
Pacific Islander	40 (67.8)	14 (23.7)	5 (8.5)	59
Middle East	7 (87.5)	0 (0.0)	1 (12.5)	8
Other	49 (75.4)	11 (16.9)	5 (7.7)	65

* Does not include the "other" category.

NEAR TRUANCY

"Near truancy" is a term used to describe behaviors that show rebellion toward attending school or class but not by being absent. In other words, near truancy behaviors are those that disturb learning, either individual learning or classroom learning. O'Keeffe points out that these behaviors are: "deliberate lateness for school or lessons, disruptive behavior in class or persistent failure to pay attention in class" (O'Keeffe, 1993, p. 29). Other versions of this phenomenon include requesting frequent trips to the restroom and excessively feigning illness.

The near truancy phenomena are elusive, but every teacher assuredly knows these types of behaviors are used solely as a strategy to avoid school and class. The student may perceive the academic work to be too rigorous or simply boring. Students may be afraid of bullies in their class or they may be afraid of their teacher. For whatever reason, students purposely try to avoid class through these "near truancy" behaviors.

Part of our truancy research included four survey items given directly to better understand near truancy. The participants were asked to respond to these four items using a Likert Scale: The responses on the Likert scale were: 5 – strongly agree, 4 – agree, 3 – neutral, 2 – disagree, 1 – strongly disagree. We compared the truants and nontruants after combining the "agree" and "strongly agree" responses. In other words, we combined the "4" and "5" responses that show agreement and the "2" and "1" responses that show disagreement.

The four statements participants responded to were: "I am sometimes late for class because I want to be with my friends," "I sometimes deliberately misbehave in class to disrupt a lesson," "I sometimes daydream in class and miss a lot of what is going on," and "I sometimes do not pay attention in class." The results are shown in table 5.6.

Since school is largely a social institution, a place where young people go to be with friends, we may logically assume truants and nontruants would sacrifice class time on occasion to be with friends.

As can be seen from the data in table 5.6, the Caucasian truants agreed with this statement more than twice as much as the Caucasian nontruants, and the ethnic minority truants agreed with this statement nearly twice as much as the ethnic minority nontruants. Of the 1,204 Caucasian truants, 626 (52.0%) were late for class because they wanted to be with friends,

Table 5.6. Caucasian/ethnic minority and truant/nontruant near truancy behavior.

	Caucasian Truants n=1204 (%)	Caucasian Nontruants n=730 (%)	Ethnic Minority Truants* n=494 (%)	Ethnic Minority Nontruants* n=198 (%)
"I am sometimes late for class because I want to be with my friends."	626 (52.0)	167 (22.9)	226 (45.7)	48 (24.2)
"I sometimes deliberately misbehave in class to disrupt a lesson."	251 (20.8)	68 (9.3)	100 (20.2)	26 (13.1)
"I sometimes daydream in class and miss a lot of what is going on."	759 (63.0)	297 (40.7)	271 (54.9)	72 (36.4)
"I sometimes do not pay attention in class."	800 (66.4)	328 (44.9)	280 (56.7)	76 (38.4)

* Does not include the "other" category.

and of the 730 Caucasian nontruants, 167 (22.9%) were late for class because of being with friends.

A smaller percentage of ethnic minority truants agreed with this statement than the Caucasian truants. Of the 494 minority truants, 226 (45.7%) agreed, and of the 198 minority nontruants, 48 (24.2%) agreed.

Another statement in this section of the survey was "I sometimes deliberately misbehave in class to disrupt a lesson." Although we would expect to see lower percentages of students engaging in this blatant disruptive behavior, the number of students who agreed was surprising. Of the 1,204 Caucasian truants, 251 (20.8%) admitted that they sometimes deliberately misbehave in class to disrupt a lesson.

The percentage of ethnic minority truants who agreed with this statement was only slightly less. Of the 494 truants, 100 (20.2%) said they sometimes deliberately disrupted lessons. This finding suggests the type of deviant behavior attributed to traditional characteristics of truants, meaning that the remainder of the truants are not malicious in their behavior. However, surprisingly, even some of the nontruants admitted that they sometimes deliberately misbehaved. Of the 730 Caucasian nontruants, 68 (9.3%) agreed with this statement, and of the 198 ethnic minority nontruants, 26 (13.1%) said they agreed.

The highest percentage of students from the specific ethnic minority groups who agreed with this statement were among the African American truants and Pacific Islander truants. Of the 41 African American truants, 18 (43.9%) said they deliberately misbehaved in class, and of the 59 Pacific Islander truants, 17 (28.8%) said they deliberately misbehaved in class.

Another form of near truancy behavior is daydreaming in class. Of course, most, if not all, students have engaged in daydreaming during class. Be that as it may, not every one of the participants admitted to daydreaming. Hopefully, it is because they feel that they do not miss *a lot* of what is going on. Of the 1,204 Caucasian truants, 759 (63.0%) said they daydream in class and miss much of the lesson. Of the 494 ethnic minority truants, 271 (54.9%) said they daydream in class.

Almost 8.0% more Caucasian truants engage in this behavior than ethnic minority truants. The Caucasian percentage is higher among nontruants as well. Of the 730 Caucasian nontruants, 297 (40.7%) said they daydream in class and miss a lot of the lesson, and of the 198 ethnic minority nontruants, 72 (36.4%) said they daydream in class and miss a lot of what is going on.

The final statement regarding near truancy was "I sometimes do not pay attention in class." Of the 1,204 Caucasian truants, 800 (66.4%) admitted that they sometimes do not pay attention in class, and of the 494 ethnic minority truants, 280 (56.7%) said that they sometimes do not pay attention in class. Clearly, over half of the truants agreed with this statement. In addition, of the 730 Caucasian nontruants, 328 (44.9%) admitted that they sometimes do not pay attention in class, while 76 (38.4%) of the 198 ethnic minority nontruants admitted to sometimes tuning out.

The obvious hypothesis is that truants are more likely to engage in near truancy behavior than nontruants. This study compared the near truancy behavior of three groups: Caucasian truants to ethnic minority truants, Caucasian nontruants to ethnic minority nontruants, and ethnic minority truants to ethnic minority nontruants. Interesting results appeared when t-tests were applied.

Table 5.7 shows the results of the responses for the statement, "I am sometimes late for class because I want to be with my friends."

The mean level of agreement on the Likert scale for Caucasian truants was 3.4 (SD 1.42), and the mean for ethnic minority truants was 3.2 (SD

Table 5.7. Simple statistics for near truancy among students who are sometimes tardy because they want to be with friends.

Group	n	Mean Score	SD
Caucasian truants	1204	3.4	1.42
Caucasian nontruants	730	2.3	1.40
Ethnic truants	494	3.2	1.49
Ethnic nontruants	198	2.5	1.41

T-test for comparing the hypothesis that Caucasian truants are *more* likely to be tardy because they want to be with friends than are ethnic truants, that Caucasian nontruants are *more* likely to be late because they want to be with friends than are ethnic nontruants, and ethnic truants are *more* likely to be late because they want to be with friends than are ethnic nontruants.

Test for Students with Near Truancy	T-Stat	P-Value
Caucasian truants greater than ethnic truants	2.88	.0020*
Caucasian nontruants greater than ethnic nontruants	−1.07	.1424
Ethnic truants greater than ethnic nontruants	6.06	.0000*

* Indicates significance at or beyond <0.05.

1.49). The difference was significant at the .0020 level. The mean for the Caucasian nontruants was 2.3 (SD 1.40) compared to 2.5 (SD 1.41) for ethnic minority nontruants. This difference was not significant at p = .1424. The difference between the mean for the ethnic minority truants and nontruants was highly significant beyond the <.05 level (p < .0001). Overall, as was expected, the means for the nontruants of both categories were lower, showing a lower level of agreement.

Table 5.8 shows the results when a t-test was applied to the responses of the statement "I sometimes deliberately misbehave in class to disrupt a lesson."

Again, we see a highly significant difference (t = 3.92, p < .0001) when comparing ethnic minority truants and nontruants in response to this item. Ethnic minority truants report that they are more likely to deliberately misbehave in class to disrupt a lesson. We also see a significant difference when comparing the Caucasian nontruants (mean 1.7, SD 1.09) to ethnic minority nontruants (mean 1.9, SD 1.27). The difference was significant at the .05 level (p = .0390). The ethnic minority nontruants are more likely to deliberately misbehave than Caucasian nontruants.

Another item on the survey designed to determine a student's propensity to engage in near truancy behavior was "I sometimes do not pay at-

Table 5.8. Simple statistics for near truancy among students who sometimes deliberately misbehave in class.

Group	n	Mean Score	SD
Caucasian truants	1204	2.3	1.36
Caucasian nontruants	730	1.7	1.09
Ethnic truants	494	2.3	1.38
Ethnic nontruants	198	1.9	1.27

T-test for comparing the hypothesis that Caucasian truants are *more* likely to deliberately misbehave in class than are ethnic truants, that Caucasian nontruants are *more* likely to deliberately misbehave in class than are ethnic nontruants, and ethnic truants are *more* likely to deliberately misbehave in class than are ethnic nontruants.

Test for Students with Deliberately Misbehaving in Class	T-Stat	P-Value
Caucasian truants greater than ethnic truants	0.21	.4161
Caucasian nontruants greater than ethnic nontruants	−1.76	.0390*
Ethnic truants greater than ethnic nontruants	3.92	.0000*

* Indicates significance at or beyond <0.05.

Table 5.9. Simple statistics for students who sometimes do not pay attention in class.

Group	n	Mean Score	SD
Caucasian truants	1204	3.8	1.23
Caucasian nontruants	730	3.1	1.33
Ethnic truants	494	3.5	1.34
Ethnic nontruants	198	2.9	1.36

T-test for comparing the hypothesis that Caucasian truants are *more* likely to not pay attention in class than are ethnic truants, that Caucasian nontruants are *more* likely to not pay attention in class than are ethnic nontruants, and ethnic truants are *more* likely to not pay attention in class than are ethnic nontruants.

Test for Students with Do Not Pay Attention in Class	T-Stat	P-Value
Caucasian truants greater than ethnic truants	3.78	.0001*
Caucasian nontruants greater than ethnic nontruants	1.20	.1153
Ethnic truants greater than ethnic nontruants	4.78	.0000*

* Indicates significance at or beyond <0.05.

tention in class." As expected, a higher mean score exists for truants than for nontruants. Table 5.9 shows the results of the t-test.

Two comparisons showed up as being significant. The mean score for Caucasian truants was 3.8 (SD 1.23), and the mean score for ethnic minority students was 3.5 (SD 1.34), a significant difference beyond the <.05 level (p = .0001). Caucasian truants are less likely to pay attention in class than ethnic minority truants.

In addition, the difference between the mean scores of the ethnic minority truants and ethnic minority nontruants was also significant (p < .0001). The statistic that should cause us to shake our heads, however, is the high mean scores of the Caucasian nontruants and the ethnic nontruants. The mean score suggests that some nontruants report that they do not pay attention in class on occasion, perhaps being there physically but not mentally.

Near truancy is manifested by actions that distract from academic learning for the student and his or her peers yet do not physically absent the truant from school or class. The percentages among truants and nontruants admitting to near truancy behavior suggest that many students are seriously disengaging themselves from classroom learning.

Statistically, we find that the difference between truants deliberately participating in near truancy behavior and nontruants participating in those behaviors is significant. However, the relatively high percentages of nontruants who agreed with these statements are very worrying, and perhaps many of these near truants are on the road to actual truancy.

REFERENCES

Guare, Rita & Bruce S. Cooper. (2003). *Truancy Revisited: Students as School Consumers*. Maryland: Scarecrow Press, Inc., 2003.

O'Keeffe, D. (1993). *Truancy in English secondary schools: A report prepared for the DFE*. London: HMSO.

Shute, J. W. (2009). *Expanding the truancy debate: Truancy, ethnic minorities and English language learners*. In M. Conolly and D. O'Keeffe (Eds.), *Don't Fence Me In: Essays on the Rational Truant* (pp. 115–38). Buckingham, England: The University of Buckingham Press.

Chapter Six

Listening to the Truants

Students are the best source of information as to why they truant. Granted, they may be unable to articulate precisely why they choose to truant from class or school, but asking them about their truancy patterns is a good first step. We can then glean from their responses what sorts of reasons were good enough to cause them to turn their backs on particular classes or entire days of school.

Our research on truancy includes aspects about students' perspectives toward items relating to their academic classes, perceived prejudices, social factors, stated lack of ability, home situations, teacher-related behaviors, and concerns with classes or schoolwork.

As part of this research, the truants were given statements and asked to agree with them by checking the appropriate box. The truants were allowed to agree with as many statements as they felt applied to them. For example, to determine which classes truants were more likely to skip, we allowed them to select as many classes as they wanted from the list of choices given to them (e.g. math, P.E., English, history, science, and electives). Responses were then tallied as a number of times each option was selected.

TRUANCY AND ACADEMIC CLASSES

Students first responded to items related to their academic classes. Finding out students' perceptions toward which academic classes they like or dislike would benefit the quest for truancy solutions. The main prelude to each statement the students were given was: "I sometimes cut school or class because . . ." followed by "I want to cut math," "I want to cut P.E.,"

"I want to cut English," and so on for history, science, and elective. As mentioned previously, students had the choice of checking all of the options that applied to them. In other words, the students were not limited to only one choice.

The data were analyzed according to Caucasian truants and ethnic minority truants. The order of which classes the 1,204 Caucasian truants favored missing were: Elective class with 352 responses, math with 319, English with 239, science with 202, P.E. with 183 responses, and history with 182 responses. Keep in mind that students could select more than one academic class. Interestingly, the favorite subject for cutting was the elective class. Apparently, these truants felt that their elective class was not worth attending consistently.

We may readily agree with math and English being favorite classes to truant from due to difficulty or language ability. However, history can be difficult and requires a decent command of the English language. We must presume, in this case, that history is an interesting class since it received the least amount of votes for classes from which to truant. We must also presume that something is happening in all the academic classes (or school in general) for each academic subject to be selected.

The responses for the 494 ethnic minority truants revealed a different order preference for classes favored from which to truant: math with 149 responses, English with 114, history with 96, science with 89, elective with 88, and P.E. with 57 responses. In addition, math and English were the top two most preferred classes to cut for each of the specific groups of minority truants who responded (i.e., Hispanic, Asian, and African American).

For purposes of this research, English, math, science, and history classes were grouped into the category "academic" classes, and P.E. and elective classes were grouped together. Table 6.1 shows the results when the t-test was applied comparing academic and P.E./elective classes.

The analysis shows that 48.2% (SD .50) of the ethnic truants reported they truant because they want to miss an academic class, whereas only 22.7% (SD .42) truant because they want to miss a P.E./elective class. The t-test showed this is a highly significant difference beyond the $<.05$ level ($p < .0001$). When cutting a class, ethnic students favor cutting academic classes over their other classes.

We can quickly see that these percentages do not equal 100%. The explanation for this is that while there were 494 truants, the categories they were

Table 6.1. Simple statistics for truancy among ethnic students as measured by classes most likely to cut (academic subjects, P.E./elective subjects).

Group	n	Truancy Level	SD
Academic Subjects	494	48.2%	0.50
P.E./Electives	494	22.7%	0.42

T-test for comparing hypothesis that ethnic students are *more* likely to truant from *academic* subjects than *P.E./elective* subjects.

Test for Ethnic Students with Types of Subjects	T-Stat	P-Value
Academic subjects more likely than P.E./ elective subjects	8.69	.0000*

* Indicates significance at or beyond <0.05.

presented with were not independent. Of these 494 truants, 238 (48.2%) said they cut because they wanted to miss an academic class. These 238 students consist of 163 truants who said they cut because they wanted to miss academic classes *only* and 75 truants who said they also cut because they wanted to miss a P.E. or elective class *in addition to academic classes*.

In other words, these 75 truants said they wanted to miss *both* P.E./elective classes and academic classes. Likewise, 112 (22.7%) truants said that they cut because they wanted to miss a P.E. or elective class. These 112 truants are comprised of 37 truants who said they cut because they wanted to miss P.E. or elective classes *only* and 75 truants who cut because they wanted to miss *both* P.E./elective classes and academic classes. Thus some overlap of the students exists.

The high levels of truancy from English and math—if they are a faithful representation of national trends—constitute a disaster that simply cannot be allowed to continue. This kind of information is eloquent proof of the enormous value of truancy data. This information also raises questions about the pedagogy, perceived usefulness of the class, textbooks, and assessments to uncover why these classes are the most popular ones these truants want to miss.

TRUANCY AND TEACHER-RELATED BEHAVIORS

Six questions in this section of the survey were designed to understand the effect certain teacher-related behaviors have on truancy. We have seen that the majority of the truants in this study favor class truancy, cutting specific classes after having arrived at the school building. Judging by the results, these teacher-related issues seem to have stirred the pot of emotions among the ethnic groups participating in this survey.

We see that teachers play a large role in the truants' desire to cut class. Just like the earlier statements, the prelude to these questions was "I sometimes cut school or class because . . ." followed by "I want to avoid particular teachers," "my teachers insult me," "my teachers are sarcastic or rude," "my teachers are unfair," "my teachers embarrass me in front of others," and "my teachers don't understand the material."

Keep in mind, again, that the truants had the choice of selecting more than one item. We have inserted table 6.2 to illustrate the results.

The first statement was "I sometimes cut school or class because I want to avoid particular teachers." By far, this item received the most agreement among the Caucasian truants as well as the ethnic minority truants. Of the 1,204 Caucasian truants, 302 (25.1%) said they might indeed cut school or class to avoid a particular teacher. This cause is more than double than that of any other items.

Table 6.2. Truancy, ethnicity, and problems with teacher interaction.

	Total Students	Total Truants (%)	Avoid Teachers (%)	Insult (%)	Rude (%)	Unfair (%)	Embarrass (%)	Material (%)
Caucasian	1934	1204	302	132	136	123	94	118
		(62.3)	(25.1)	(11.0)	(11.3)	(10.2)	(7.8)	(9.8)
Minority Groups*	692	494	138	65	100	80	55	60
		(71.4)	(27.9)	(13.2)	(20.2)	(16.2)	(11.1)	(12.1)
Hispanic	361	279	80	37	58	43	31	34
		(77.3)	(28.7)	(13.3)	(20.8)	(15.4)	(11.1)	(12.2)
African American	56	41	12	10	13	14	10	11
		(73.2)	(29.3)	(24.4)	(31.7)	(34.1)	(24.4)	(26.8)
Asian	132	76	14	4	9	7	3	8
		(57.6)	(18.4)	(5.3)	(11.8)	(9.2)	(3.9)	(10.5)
Native American	42	31	9	4	4	1	3	2
		(73.8)	(29.0)	(12.9)	(12.9)	(3.2)	(9.7)	(6.5)
Pacific Islander	88	59	22	10	16	15	8	5
		(67.0)	(37.3)	(16.9)	(27.1)	(25.4)	(13.6)	(8.5)
Middle East	13	8	1	0	0	0	0	0
		(61.5)	(12.5)	(0.0)	(0.0)	(0.0)	(0.0)	(0.0)
Other	101	65	20	16	16	13	10	11
		(64.4)	(30.8)	(24.6)	(24.6)	(20.0)	(15.4)	(16.9)

* Does not include the "other" category.

Similarly, of the 494 ethnic minority truants, 138 (27.9%) said they would cut school or class to avoid a particular teacher, also higher than the other items. But why do these truants want to avoid particular teachers? For possible reasons, we need to look at the next five statements.

These next statements were designed to determine if the truants felt that teachers insulted them, were rude, were unfair, or embarrassed the students in class, or if the truant felt that the teacher did not understand the material being taught. Understandably, any of these teacher behaviors would be a legitimate cause for any student to want to cut school or class.

Of the 1,204 Caucasian truants, 132 (11.0%) said they would cut school or class if the teacher insulted them, 136 (11.3%) said they would truant if the teacher was rude, 123 (10.2%) said they would truant if the teacher was unfair, 94 (7.8%) said they would truant if the teacher embarrassed them, and 118 (9.8%) indicated they would truant if they felt the teacher did not understand the material.

Interestingly, since 25% of the responses indicated that these Caucasian truants want to avoid teachers, apparently they do so for reasons not necessarily listed in this section of the survey.

We see slightly higher percentages for the ethnic minority truants for all five of the other statements. Of the 494 ethnic minority truants, 65 (13.2%) said they were likely to truant from school or class if the teacher insulted them, 100 (20.2%) said they would truant if the teacher was rude, 80 (16.2%) said they would truant if the teacher was unfair, 55 (11.1%) said they would truant if the teacher embarrassed them, and 60 (12.1%) said they would truant if they felt that the teacher did not know the material.

However, these results still suggest that other reasons are at work as to why ethnic minority students want to truant to avoid particular teachers. These behavioral issues obviously play a role in both Caucasian and ethnic minority students' propensity to be truant, but other issues such as individual teaching styles and personalities could affect the students.

A few points are worth mentioning regarding the results from the specific ethnic groups. First, it was the Pacific Islanders who felt the strongest about avoiding particular teachers. Of the 59 Pacific Islander truants, 22 (37.3%) said they would truant to avoid a particular teacher. Their percentages are higher across the other items as well. Of the 59 truants, 10 (16.9%) would truant if their teacher insulted them, 16

(27.1%) would truant if the teacher was rude, 15 (25.4%) would truant if the teacher was unfair, and 8 (13.6%) said they would truant if the teacher embarrassed them.

Although the percentages for the Pacific Islander truants are high, they are not as high as the results from the African American truants, except with the case of avoiding particular teachers. Of the 41 African American truants, 10 (24.4%) said they would truant from school or class if the teacher insulted them, 13 (31.7%) said they would truant if the teacher was rude, 14 (34.1%) said they would truant if the teacher was unfair, 10 (24.4%) said they would truant if the teacher embarrassed them, and 11 (26.8%) said they would be absent if the teacher did not know the material.

These percentages are much higher than the average for all ethnic minority truants. These results are incredibly disturbing, and untangling the complex issues involved would be challenging. One might wonder if the difficulty of the challenge to look at truancy specifically in relation to teacher behaviors, curriculum, and pedagogy is precisely the reason it is avoided.

TRUANCY AND CONCERNS WITH CLASSES OR SCHOOLWORK

In addition to asking students if they truant because of teacher-related behaviors, we also inquired if students truant because of concerns with their classes or schoolwork. As with the other questions in this part of the survey, the prelude was "I sometimes cut school or class because . . ." followed by "I need to finish homework," "I want to avoid particular subjects," "I do not like some of my classes," "I am unprepared for or frightened of an exam," and "the lessons seem to be of no use for me." The truants had the option of choosing more than one item.

Again, a table listing the responses is useful. We have included table 6.3 to show the results.

While teacher behaviors were shown to be a reason for truancy, the percentages in all of these categories are higher than the percentages of previous categories. In addition, the percentages of the Caucasians and ethnic minorities were strikingly similar.

Table 6.3. Truancy among ethnic groups because of concerns with classes or schoolwork.

	Total Students	Total Truants (%)	Doing Homework (%)	Avoiding Subjects (%)	Disliking Classes (%)	Avoiding Exam (%)	Lessons of No Use (%)
Caucasian	1934	1204	464	273	577	216	296
		(62.3)	(38.5)	(22.7)	(47.9)	(17.9)	(24.6)
Minority Groups*	692	494	187	129	243	92	99
		(71.4)	(37.9)	(26.1)	(49.2)	(18.6)	(20.0)
Hispanic	361	279	95	76	150	42	54
		(77.3)	(34.1)	(27.4)	(53.8)	(15.1)	(19.4)
African American	56	41	11	18	19	13	15
		(73.2)	(26.8)	(43.9)	(46.3)	(31.7)	(36.6)
Asian	132	76	42	17	29	14	13
		(57.6)	(55.3)	(22.4)	(38.2)	(18.4)	(17.1)
Native American	42	31	11	6	13	5	8
		(73.8)	(35.5)	(19.4)	(41.9)	(16.1)	(25.8)
Pacific Islander	88	59	25	11	32	17	7
		(67.0)	(42.4)	(18.6)	(54.2)	(28.8)	(11.9)
Middle East	13	8	3	1	0	1	2
		(61.5)	(37.5)	(12.5)	(0.0)	(12.5)	(25.0)
Other	101	65	29	13	30	10	19
		(64.4)	(44.6)	(20.0)	(46.2)	(15.4)	(19.2)

* Does not include the "other" category.

As shown in table 6.3, "dislike of classes" was the most agreed upon reason for cutting school or class among the items in this section of the survey for both Caucasian truants and ethnic minority truants. Of the 1,204 Caucasian truants, 577 (47.9%) said they sometimes truant because they do not like some of their classes, and of the 494 ethnic minority truants, 243 (49.2%) stated likewise. Clearly, a dislike of some classes is a big reason why students truant.

Interestingly, the reason that received the second highest number of responses for sometimes truanting is that truants need to finish their homework. Of the 1,204 Caucasian truants, 464 (38.5%) gave this as a reason why they would sometimes truant from school or class and of the 494 ethnic minority truants, 187 (37.9%) said they would truant for the same reason.

Previous research on truancy has claimed that truants are juvenile delinquents with nothing better to do than skip school and commit crimes while on drugs. This notion has been contended in this current research, and here again we see that a large percentage of truants, both Caucasian and from ethnic minority groups, cut school or class to finish homework.

While there is widespread alienation from the curriculum and peda-gogy, the situation is very ambiguous because curriculum and pedagogy clearly do engage the students' attention: hence, the strong connection between truancy and finishing homework. Truancy, it would seem, has its functional side.

Of course, we must wonder why many truants cut class to finish their homework in the first place. Perhaps these students need help with their time management and organization. The fact remains, however, that they are truanting for the "commendable" reason of finishing homework.

With regard to the specific ethnic groups, we continue to see a higher percentage in each item among African Americans, with the exception of the reason of finishing homework as a motivation to truant. The inter-esting point is that of the five reasons for truancy listed in table 6.3, the one that is lowest for the African Americans is very high for all the other ethnic races.

For the statement "I sometimes cut school or class because I need to finish my homework," 34.1% of the Hispanic, 55.3% of the Asian (the highest), 35.5% of the Native American, 42.4% of the Pacific Islander, and 37.5% of the Middle Eastern truants agreed. But for the 41 African Americans, 11 (26.8%) agreed with this "homework" statement.

The huge percentage among the Asian truants in response to this state-ment is interesting in that it is not only the highest percentage on this table, but it is the highest percentage on all of the preceding tables report-ing data in this section of the survey. Apparently, the Asian truants feel very strongly that finishing their homework is an important reason to cut school or class.

Another group of high percentages among all the ethnic groups is for the statement "I sometimes cut school or class because I do not like some of my classes," with the exception of the Middle Eastern truants. But for these other ethnic groups, 53.8% of the Hispanic, 46.3% of the African American, 38.2% of the Asian, 41.9% of the Native American, and 54.2% of the Pacific Islander truants agreed with this statement.

Clearly, the truants from these different ethnic groups felt very strongly about this statement. Again, these are some of the highest percentages in this section of the survey, suggesting that emotions run high with respect to liking and disliking class as reasons for truancy.

Another interesting point is the relatively low percentage of agreement with the statement "I sometimes cut school or class because the lessons seem to be of no use to me." We might expect that more of the truants would agree with this statement since they appear to absent themselves from classes quite often. In other words, if students believe that the lessons are of use to them, then their truancy levels ought to be lower. For the purpose of this research, we must live with this ambiguity.

TRUANCY AND STATED LACK OF ABILITY

The survey also contained questions related to the truants' ability to understand their lessons, understand English, and whether they read well. The intent was to discover if any of these have a bearing on their propensity to truant. The three items in this section of the survey had the same prelude as before: "I sometimes cut school or class because . . ." followed by "I do not understand some of the lessons," "I do not understand English well," and "I do not read well." The students had the choice of checking all that applied specifically to them, hence they were not limited to only one choice.

Here again, we see quite a large difference between the Caucasian percentages and the percentages from the ethnic minorities in all three topics. Of the 1,204 Caucasian truants, 160 (13.3%) responded that they truanted because they didn't understand some of the lessons. The ethnic minority responses were almost double that of the Caucasian responses. Of the 494 truants, 125 (25.3%) agreed that they would cut school or class because they do not understand the lessons.

The trend continues for the next two topics although the percentages of agreement were quite low. Of the 1,204 Caucasians, only 34 (2.8%) said they would cut school or class because they do not understand English well, but of the 494 students belonging to ethnic minorities, 40 (8.1%) (although a low percentage, it is four times the percentage of Caucasians) said they would cut school or class for the same reason.

Virtually the same pattern exists for the statement "I sometimes cut school or class because I do not read well." Of the 1,204 Caucasian truants, 36 (3.0%) said they would truant, and of the 494 ethnic minority truants, 41 (8.3%) said they would truant.

The high percentages found in each specific ethnic group for the statement about cutting school or class because of not understanding some of the lessons are also interesting. The African Americans held the highest percentages for all three statements, 34.1%, 24.4%, and 22.0%, respectively. The fact that African Americans struggle with English and that these reasons warrant truancy for *any* student are noteworthy and tragic.

Of course, the fact that any student would purposely cut class because they did not understand some of the lesson is appalling and unacceptable for any teacher. We must ask ourselves if these particular 285 students are juvenile delinquents, up to no good, or students rejecting the class on grounds of poor teaching in these particular classes.

This is not to say that all teaching is bad. However, these students are truanting because they don't understand the lessons, which indicates that blame, in this case, must be shared by the teachers.

TRUANCY AND PERCEIVED PREJUDICE

Another topic of importance is that of truancy for reasons of perceived prejudice. Students were offered the opportunity to give their thoughts about prejudices regarding their gender, religion, and race. In other words, we wanted to know if students specifically cut class because they felt prejudice toward them. As with the previous item on the survey, students had the choice of checking all that applied to them.

The main prelude to each statement was "I sometimes cut school or class because . . ." followed by "I feel harassed because of my gender," "I feel harassed because of my religion," and "I feel harassed because of my race."

Interestingly, the responses for these items were surprisingly low for both Caucasian and ethnic minority truants. Of the 1,204 Caucasian truants, 36 (3.0%) of the responses indicated that the truant cut class as a result of feeling harassed because of their gender, another 37 (3.1%) responses because of their religion, and 36 (3.0%) because of their race.

Although the response rates are higher for these statements among the ethnic minority students, they are still very low. Of the 494 ethnic minority truants, 29 (5.9%) responses indicated that they truant as a result of feeling harassed because of their gender, another 25 (5.1%) responses indicated they cut class because of their religion, and 56 (11.3%) because of their race. For the most part, these percentages were not drastically different than that of their Caucasian counterparts, but they were still higher.

Another piece of interesting data is the high percentages for all statements found among African Americans. Of the 41 African American truants, 11 (26.8%) responses indicated that the truant cut class as a result of feeling harassed because of their gender, 10 (24.4%) because of their religion, and 17 (41.5%) because of their race.

These percentages are all higher than any other ethnic group. In fact, for the statement regarding cutting class because of perceived "racial" prejudice, the African American percentage of 41.5% is 32.2 percentage points higher than the next closest group's percentage. The overall number of African American truants (n=41) is hardly enough to make any real conclusions; however, the extremely high percentage of responses to this statement is interesting.

Obviously, according to these data, one might conclude that the ethnic minority truants, with the exception of African American students, felt very little prejudice toward them as a reason for their truancy.

TRUANCY AND SOCIAL FACTORS

Another goal of this research was to look at the social nature of truancy. In other words, do students truant because their friends truant? Two main items in this section of the survey are related to friends. As in previous examples, the prelude to each question was "I sometimes cut school or class because . . ." followed by "I don't have friends in some classes" and "my friends do, and they ask me to come." As with the previous items, students had the choice of checking all that applied to them.

While the previous two sections found different results for Caucasian and ethnic minority truants, the percentages for these two items are remarkably similar. Of the 1,204 Caucasian truants, 182 (15.1%) said they would sometimes cut school or class because they did not have friends in the class. The usage of "would" here is intended to mean "might well be inclined to." Similarly, of the 494 ethnic minority truants, 65 (13.2%), said they would cut school or class for that reason. Neither of these percentages is all that high compared to the next question.

Of the 1,204 Caucasian truants, 492 (40.9%) said they would cut school or class because their friends do and ask them to come along. Similarly, of the 494 ethnic minority truants, 196 (39.7%) said they would sometimes truant from school or class if their friends did and asked them to. These percentages are extremely close for both groups and are more than double that of the previous item.

TRUANCY AND HOME SITUATIONS

Home situations have always been a scapegoat for the students' truancy problem. This item on the survey was designed to find out if home situations had a bearing on truancy. As with previous items, the prelude to this question was "I sometimes cut school or class because . . ." followed by "of a home situation." Again, all truants had the option to choose more than one item. This item on their home situation could have been chosen along with other items in this section.

Truants from ethnic minority groups responded in the affirmative to this statement over the Caucasian truants. Of the 1,204 Caucasian truants, 180 (15.0%) said they would sometimes cut school or class because of a home situation. Of the 494 ethnic minority truants, an even 100 (20.2%) said they would cut school or class because of a situation at home.

Again, a greater percentage of African Americans selected this reason than any other ethnic minority group. Of the 41 African American truants, 12 (29.3%) said they would cut class or school because of a situation at home. The second highest percentage came from the Pacific Islander truants. Of these 59 truants, 14 (23.7%) stated they would truant because of a home situation. Hispanic truants also agreed. Of these 279 truants, 57 (20.4%) would cut school or class for home reasons. Native Americans were at 16.1% and Asians were at 15.8%.

While home situations obviously affect some truants, this condition does not have as much of a bearing on their truancy behavior as other reasons appear to have, including the previous item of truanting because of not understanding the lesson. Clearly, other factors besides home situations are at work to motivate students into truancy.

Of course, the "home situations" reason leaves some room for interpretation. Do these "home situations" involve dysfunctional parents and a complete lack of supervision, or do these "home situations" involve parental demand for babysitters, shopkeepers, or other reasons? In other words, not all "home situations" are negative.

TRUANCY AND PERCEIVED VALUE OF EDUCATION

As we better understand truants' values toward different aspects of education, we may better determine why they truant. If students *do not* value education as something beneficial and useful for their lives, we could perhaps understand why truants absented themselves away from education opportunities—they don't like it and therefore don't attend.

If students *do* value education as something beneficial and useful and purposely absent themselves away from an education opportunity, we must infer that something of equal or greater value is pulling students away. We must then be open to all possibilities, including drugs, psychological problems, and family, as well as teacher behavior, dislike of lessons, and boring lessons.

This part of the research included statements to which the participants responded by stating their level of agreement on a Likert scale: circling a "1" meant that the students "strongly disagreed" with the statement, circling a "2" meant that the students "somewhat disagreed," circling a "3" meant that the students were "neutral" regarding that statement, circling a "4" meant that the students "somewhat agreed," and circling a "5" meant that the students "strongly agreed" with the statement.

For our purposes here, we combined the "4" and "5" responses since both denoted agreement to the statement. We then compared the truant and nontruant responses for Caucasian and ethnic minority students. As with the data in the previous section, the ethnic minority group total does not include students who are in the "other" category for reasons previously stated.

TRUANCY AND VALUE OF EDUCATION

Asking students for their opinions regarding the importance of education can be useful in making inferences regarding their reasons for truancy (e.g., are they rebelling against education and learning in general or rebelling against another aspects of education and learning?).

The following three statements were given: "I believe that gaining an education will improve the quality of my life," "education is something that is important in my home," and "I want to continue with higher education after high school." Understandably, most people would agree that education is of value, and in this study the majority of Caucasian and ethnic minority truants and nontruants agreed with uncanny similarity. Table 6.4 shows students' responses.

Seemingly, truants and nontruants have the same view regarding these aspects of education since both truants and nontruants overwhelmingly agreed with these statements. For example, of the 1,204 Caucasian truants, 1,106 (91.9%) agreed that education will improve the quality of their life, and of the 730 Caucasian nontruants, 706 (96.7%) agreed with this statement.

Table 6.4.   Caucasian/ethnic minority and truant/nontruant opinions about education.

	Caucasian Truants n=1204 (%)	Caucasian Nontruants n=730 (%)	Ethnic Minority Truants* n=494 (%)	Ethnic Minority Nontruants* n=198 (%)
"I believe gaining an education will improve the quality of my life."	1106 (91.9)	706 (96.7)	452 (91.5)	191 (96.5)
"Education is something that is important in my home."	1085 (90.1)	694 (95.1)	447 (90.5)	185 (93.4)
"I want to continue with higher education after high school."	1042 (86.5)	693 (94.9)	416 (84.2)	181 (91.4)

* Does not include the "other" category.

Similarly, of the 494 minority truants, 452 (91.5%) agreed that education will improve their quality of life, and of the 198 minority nontruants, 191 (96.5%) agreed with this statement. The same high percentages exist for the responses for the other two statements.

Clearly, both truants and nontruants agree that education will improve the quality of their lives and is important in their homes, and that they have a desire to continue with higher education after high school.

However, although these truants firmly believe that education in principle is a major source of human benefit, the truants purposely took themselves away from school classes. The obvious question is "why are these students truanting in such large numbers if they believe that getting an education will improve their lives?" One possibility, of course, is that truants reject individual classes rather than education on the whole. Indeed, the conviction that this is so among confessed truants seems astonishingly high.

The overall truancy level of 62.3% for Caucasian students and 71.4% for ethnic minority (table 5.3) students suggests that a large majority of the students do not feel that their present schooling situation is of value. Perhaps the schools they are attending or the classes they are taking are ones that do not fit their scheme of an important education.

We acknowledge that other reasons for truancy exist; however, we must also acknowledge that it is very likely that these students truant because they are not equating their present education to the kind of education that will improve their quality of life. With such high percentages of both truants and nontruants agreeing with this statement, the incidence of truancy in these high schools is disturbing.

The lowest percentages (although still high percentages) from the responses occurred for the statement "I want to continue with higher education after high school." Of the 1,204 Caucasian truants, 1,042 (86.5%) agreed that they wanted to continue with higher education after high school, whereas of the 730 Caucasian nontruants, 693 (94.9%) agreed.

Of the 494 ethnic minority students, 416 (84.2%) wanted to continue with higher education after high school, and of the 198 ethnic minority nontruants, 181 (91.4%) wanted to further their education after high school.

The high levels of truancy among these pupils who claim they want to go on to higher education therefore suggest that they are turned off by the individual classes and teachers in high school and not by the educational process on the whole. They are certainly not concluding that going on to college is not worthwhile.

Again, truants do not seem to be turning their backs on education as a whole. They believe that education is important, but we can infer from these high percentages that their truancy indicates a major element of criticism of the education, most likely poor curriculum and teaching, which perhaps they are offered disguised as education.

TRUANCY AND PERCEIVED PARENTAL VIEWS OF EDUCATION

Another piece of this research sought to analyze the students' perception of how their parent(s)/guardian(s) felt about school. The students responded to these statements on the survey: "my parent(s)/guardian(s) care that I do well in school" and "my parents encourage me to attend school." For both Caucasians and the ethnic minorities, the overwhelming majority agreed with this statement and believed that their parents or guardians cared that they did well in school. Table 6.5 shows these results.

As suspected, we see that an overwhelming majority of both Caucasian and ethnic minority truants and nontruants believe their parents want them to do well in school. In response to the statement "my parent(s)/ guardian(s) care that I do well in school," we see that 1,124 (93.4%) of the 1,204 Caucasian truants agreed with this statement, and 701 (96.0%) of the 730 Caucasian nontruants agreed.

Table 6.5.   Caucasian/ethnic minority and truant/nontruant opinions about perceived parental views of education.

	Caucasian Truants n=1204 (%)	Caucasian Nontruants n=730 (%)	Ethnic Minority Truants* n=494 (%)	Ethnic Minority Nontruants* n=198 (%)
"My parent(s)/guardian(s) care that I do well in school."	1124 (93.4)	701 (96.0)	455 (92.1)	188 (94.9)
"My parents encourage me to attend school."	1109 (92.1)	694 (95.1)	433 (87.7)	182 (91.9)

* Does not include the "other" category.

The responses from the ethnic minority students showed similar results. Of the 494 ethnic minority truants, 455 (92.1%) believed that their parents cared that they did well in school, while 188 (94.9%) of the 198 nontruants believed the same. Similar high percentages exist for the statement "my parents encourage me to attend school."

We must wonder why so many students continue to truant. Reasonably, most students would state that their parents cared that they did well in school. Most of the students (truants and nontruants) believed that at the very least their parents have a value system that includes education, and that their parents encourage them to attend school.

Presumably, parents want their children to do well in school. This being the case, the high truancy levels could mean that these truants simply do not feel that cutting school or class will affect their doing well in school because they continue to truant knowing their parents want them in school.

If they continue to cut class and school, they may not think truanting will have a negative effect on their education. Or, if they do think truanting will adversely affect their education, these students simply do not care about their parents' concern for them to do well. We must admit, however, that this latter possibility would be unlikely for many of the truants.

Another possibility is: if education is important to the parents, are parents communicating this to the students? From the high truancy levels, either the importance of education is not being communicated or the students are willfully going against the desires of their parents, which, of course, must be true in some cases.

Do the truants really *not* equate attendance in class with a successful education? Perhaps, for them, getting an education means testing well, and being in school or class is a formality that can be dismissed when desired. The high levels of truancy found in this study continue to seem surprising.

If the truants know that their parents encourage getting an education but continually cut school and class, a serious disconnect has occurred. The truants may know that their parents believe that getting an education is important, but they may also believe that they do not receive enough support from their parents in the form of help with homework and other projects.

Students also identified their opinion concerning these two statements: "my parents/guardians help me with my homework if I need it" and "my

Table 6.6. Caucasian/ethnic minority and truant/nontruant opinions about perceived
parental views of education.

	Caucasian Truants n=1204 (%)	Caucasian Nontruants n=730 (%)	Ethnic Minority Truants* n=494 (%)	Ethnic Minority Nontruants* n=198 (%)
"My parent(s)/guardian(s) help me with my homework if I need it."	730 (60.6)	517 (70.8)	255 (51.6)	108 (54.5)
"My parents do not know how to help me with my school work."	430 (35.7)	218 (29.9)	191 (38.7)	79 (39.9)

* Does not include the "other" category.

parents do not know how to help me with my schoolwork." Table 6.6
shows the students' responses.

While most of the truants and nontruants believed that their parents
encouraged them to do well in school, fewer of them believed that their
parents helped them when they needed it. Of the 1,204 Caucasian truants,
730 (60.6%) agreed that their parents would help them with their homework
if they needed it. Of the 730 Caucasian nontruants, 517 (70.8%) agreed that
their parents would help them with their homework. Of the 494 ethnic minority truants, 255 (51.6%) agreed that their parents would help them with
their homework, and of the 198 nontruants, 108 (54.5%) agreed.

In other words, a little less than half of the truants felt that their parents
did not help them with homework when they needed help. Perhaps parents
verbally encourage their children to attend school but do not often show
their beliefs with actions, for example, by helping with homework. Students believe that their parents do not often sacrifice much of their time
to help with homework, thus sending a message that homework really is
not that critical, and therefore school is not that important.

Many of these ethnic minority students believed that their parents encouraged them to do well in school but at the same time did not believe
that their parents displayed that encouragement by giving help with homework. We might agree that this belief would contribute to truancy levels,
but the same belief is held by the nontruants as well.

If some of the participants did not feel that their parents would help
them with their schoolwork, perhaps it was because their parents could

not help them because they did not know how to do the work. The responses to the next statement, "my parents do not know how to help me with my schoolwork," show that a higher percentage of the ethnic minority students believed this was the case. While the parental encouragement to do well in school was evident, the parental ability to help with homework was not.

The lower percentages indicate that most truants and nontruants believed that their parents were indeed capable of helping them. However, one-third of the students, truants and nontruants, agreed that their parents could not, academically, help them. In essence, many of the ethnic minority students believed their parents did not know how to do the schoolwork. This finding may be understandable, but many of the Caucasian students felt the same way.

Responses from the Caucasian and ethnic minority truants and nontruants for this statement were similar. Conversely, many truants and nontruants believed that their parents were capable of helping them with their homework. Of the 1,204 Caucasian truants, 430 (35.7%) believed that their parents did not know how to help them, while 218 (29.9%) of the 730 nontruants believed the same. Of the 494 ethnic minority truants, 191 (38.7%) believed that their parents did not know how to help them, while 79 (39.9%) of the 198 ethnic minority nontruants believed the same.

Overall, the results for the previous four statements seem to suggest that most truants and nontruants believe that their parents encourage them to do well in school but do not often show that encouragement by helping them with their homework, even though many students believe that their parents are capable of helping them.

TRUANCY AND READING LEVELS

Another function of school that we wanted to understand was the truants' view on reading. Proficiency in reading is a crucial skill to possess to ensure success in education. The students expressed to what extent they agreed with the statements: "I am a good reader," "I enjoy reading," and "reading is not important in my home." Table 6.7 shows the results.

We see a drop in percentages in the students' responses to this statement compared to the percentages found in response to the statements

Table 6.7.   Caucasian/ethnic minority and truant/nontruant opinions about reading.

	Caucasian Truants n=1204 (%)	Caucasian Nontruants n=730 (%)	Ethnic Minority Truants* n=494 (%)	Ethnic Minority Nontruants* n=198 (%)
"I am a good reader."	986 (81.9)	619 (84.8)	350 (70.9)	152 (76.8)
"I enjoy reading."	614 (51.0)	473 (64.8)	204 (41.3)	106 (53.5)
"Reading is not important in my home."	231 (19.2)	111 (15.2)	113 (22.9)	40 (20.2)

* Does not include the "other" category.

regarding the value of education, but still the percentages remain high. And surprisingly, the data show that the percentages of truants and non-truants who believe that they are good readers is remarkably similar for both Caucasian and ethnic minority students.

Of the 1,204 Caucasian truants, 986 (81.9%) believed that they were good readers, and of the 730 Caucasian nontruants, 619 (84.8%) agreed that they were good readers. A slightly larger difference exists among the ethnic minority students. Of the 494 ethnic minority truants, 350 (70.9%) agreed that they were good readers, and 152 (76.8%) of the 198 ethnic minority nontruants agreed.

Not surprisingly, however, the percentage of ethnic minority students (truants and nontruants) who considered themselves to be good readers is lower than the percentage of Caucasian truants and nontruants who considered themselves to be good readers.

We can conclude that at least in the area of reading, over half of the truants, Caucasian and ethnic minorities, considered themselves able to read well enough to be successful in school, showing their intellectual capability to read. Therefore, perhaps we can assume that all truants are not academically weak and that their truancy behavior is calculated and purposeful, for other reasons.

After indicating how they perceived their reading proficiency, students were also asked to indicate their level of agreement with the statement "I enjoy reading." A greater difference between the truants and nontruants appeared for this statement from the previous one. A smaller percentage of the Caucasian and ethnic minority truants enjoyed reading than their nontruant counterparts.

Of the 1,204 Caucasian truants, only 614 (51.0%) enjoyed reading, while 473 (64.8%) of the 730 nontruants enjoyed reading. The percentages are lower for the ethnic minority truants and nontruants. Of the 494 minority truants, only 204 (41.3%) said they enjoyed reading, and of the 198 minority nontruants, only 106 (53.5%) said they enjoyed reading.

To an educator, these percentages must be unacceptable. If students perceive they know how to read well, why don't more of them enjoy reading? While not within the scope of this research, this finding suggests a certain failure on the part of our educational enterprise. Most people would agree that if you read well, you probably enjoy reading; however, it appears that this is not the case with these students. Perhaps our focus on test scores has detoured our teaching of reading away from enjoyment.

If students believe that reading is important to their families, they are likely to read more. For the statement "reading is not important in my home," 19.2% of the Caucasian truants and 22.9% of the ethnic minority truants agreed. The lower percentages for this statement can be attributed to the fact that most students *do believe* that reading is important in their home, and the percentages are quite similar among both truants and nontruants, Caucasian and ethnic minorities. However, from an intellectual viewpoint, the percentage of students who stated that reading was not important in their homes was tragically high.

TRUANCY AND VIEWS ON FRIENDS AND EDUCATION

School is largely a social gathering for many young people, and friends are a major part of the school day. The propensity to truant for some students may be connected to truancy behavior and the view of education held by friends. Students responded to two statements: "most of my friends do well in school" and "my friends encourage me to do well in school." Table 6.8 shows the results.

These higher percentages show that students as a whole are doing well in school and claim that they perform at an average or above average level in school. But these same students who think they are "doing well in

Table 6.8. Caucasian/ethnic minority and truant/nontruant opinions about friends.

	Caucasian Truants n=1204 (%)	Caucasian Nontruants n=730 (%)	Ethnic Minority Truants* n=494 (%)	Ethnic Minority Nontruants* n=198 (%)
"Most of my friends do well in school."	781 (64.9)	545 (74.7)	298 (60.3)	142 (71.7)
"My friends encourage me to do well in school."	618 (51.3)	445 (61.0)	258 (52.2)	121 (61.1)

* Does not include the "other" category.

school" are truanting in droves. This suggests that many truants, and their friends, are not necessarily performing horribly in their classes.

Of the 1,204 Caucasian truants, 781 (64.9%) believed that most of their friends did well in school. Not surprisingly, a higher percentage, 545 (74.7%) of the 730 Caucasian nontruants, believed that their friends did well in school. Of the 494 ethnic minority truants, 298 (60.3%) believed that their friends did well in school, while 142 (71.7%) of the 198 ethnic minority nontruants thought the same.

More nontruants believed that their friends were doing well in school than truants who believed that their friends were doing well; but, again, most students, truants and nontruants, Caucasians and ethnic minorities alike, believed that their friends were doing average or above average. We can infer that many truants are not the academically challenged students that they have been stereotyped to be.

In addition to asking students if they believed that their friends were doing well in school, the survey also asked students for their perception as to whether their friends encouraged them to do well in school. The results followed a similar pattern for the Caucasian and ethnic minority truants and nontruants. The percentages show that the majority of Caucasian and ethnic minority truants and nontruants believe that their friends encourage them to do well in school.

An obvious contradiction exists in these students' perceptions—that many "friends" are truanting but at the same time encouraging each other to do well in school. Perhaps these truants do not equate truancy/attendance with doing well in school. Again, we must analyze what is happening in our classrooms for this unbalanced perception to exist.

TRUANCY AND STUDENTS' PERCEPTION
OF THEIR SCHOOL TRUANCY POLICY

Another interesting part of this study was to look at how the students view their school's attendance and truancy policy. One standard suggestion, and a logical one, on how to reduce truancy is to ensure the school has a strict truancy policy and is committed to consistently enforce it.

The statements in this section of the survey were: "my school has a strict policy on cutting or sluffing *school*," "my school has a strict policy on cutting or sluffing *class*," "my school does not enforce the attendance policy," and "in my school, it is easy to cut class." Table 6.9 shows the results of the students' responses.

The similarities of these percentages are remarkable. Most of the Caucasian truants (64.5%) and ethnic minority truants (66.8%) believed that their school had a strict policy on *school* truancy. Likewise, 63.8% of the Caucasian truants and 66.8% of the ethnic minority truants believed that their school had a strict policy on *class* cutting. Interestingly, the high truancy levels continue despite this belief.

In other words, over 60% of the truants believed that their school had a strict policy on cutting school and class, yet they still truanted. Not only do they believe that their school has a strict policy, at least 80% indicated that their school will enforce this policy. This suggests that as students

Table 6.9. Caucasian/ethnic minority and truant/nontruant opinions about their school attendance policies.

	Caucasian Truants n=1204 (%)	Caucasian Nontruants n=730 (%)	Ethnic Minority Truants* n=494 (%)	Ethnic Minority Nontruants* n=198 (%)
"My school has a strict policy on cutting or sluffing *school*."	776 (64.5)	476 (65.2)	330 (66.8)	145 (73.2)
"My school has a strict policy on cutting or sluffing *class*."	768 (63.8)	484 (66.3)	330 (66.8)	152 (76.8)
"My school does not enforce the attendance policy."	200 (16.6)	110 (15.1)	105 (21.3)	34 (17.2)
"In my school, it is easy to cut class."	660 (54.8)	322 (44.1)	241 (48.8)	83 (41.9)

* Does not include the "other" category.

truant from school and class in droves, they still believe that their school has a truancy policy that is enforced.

In addition, while the truants think that their school has a strict truancy policy, and that they believe the school enforces this policy, half of the truants believe that it is "easy" to cut class. These percentages seem high for students who believe that their school has a strict truancy policy and that their school enforces that policy.

The high percentages suggest that the students cut class because they think they can get away with it, and since they can get away with it, they spend their time doing things they believe are more important to them (perhaps homework), or, because they can get away with truancy, they spend their time *away* from their perceived rude, insulting teachers and perceived useless classes.

TRUANCY AND PARENTS' KNOWLEDGE OF CHILD'S TRUANCY

Another aspect of this study was to find out whether the truants believe that their parents knew about their truancy. The students were asked, "do either of your parent(s)/guardian(s) know that you cut?" The choices were: "no, neither knows," "yes, one or both know(s)," and "I don't know if either knows." The majority of both the Caucasian truants and the ethnic minority truants believed that their parents or guardians knew about their truanting behavior.

Of the 954 Caucasian truants who took the survey, 480 (50.3%) said they believed that one or both of their parents or guardians knew that they truanted, and 335 (35.1%) said they believed that neither parent nor guardian knew that they truanted. Of the 397 minority truants, 170 (42.8%) said they believed that one or both of their parents or guardians knew about their truanting, and 167 (42.1%) of the truants said they believed that neither of their parents knew about their truanting.

A higher percentage of truancy was found among the Hispanic truants and truants from the Pacific Islands who believed their parents did not know about their truanting. Of the 231 Hispanic truants, 100 (43.3%) believed that their parents did not know they were truanting, and 93 (40.3%) believed that at least one of their parents knew. Of the 42 truants from the

Pacific Islands, 23 (54.8%) believed that their parents did not know they truanted, while 15 (35.7%) believed that their parents did know.

Considering the massive levels of truancy revealed in these data, we are surprised to find that the students continue to truant even though they (1) value education, (2) believe that their parents value education, and (3) believe that their parents know they truant.

TRUANCY AND TEACHERS' KNOWLEDGE OF STUDENTS' TRUANCY

This survey also asked truants to indicate if they believed that their teachers knew about their truancy. The students were asked, "do any of your teachers know that you cut?" The choices given were: "no teacher knows," "at least one teacher knows," and "I don't know if any teacher knows." In relation to truants believing that their parents knew if they truanted, the opposite is true when asked if they believed that their teachers knew if they truanted. However, in this case, more truants admitted that they did not know.

Of the 1,104 Caucasian truants who responded to this item on the survey, 429 (38.9%) believed that none of their teachers knew they truanted, 354 Caucasian truants (32.1%) were not sure if their teachers knew, and 321 (29.1%) thought that at least one of their teachers knew. The same pattern exists for the minority truants. Of the 461 minority truants who responded to this item, 195 (42.3%) believed that none of their teachers knew they truanted, 146 (31.7%) were not sure if their teachers knew, and 120 (26.0%) thought that none of their teachers knew.

Again, we are surprised to find that even though more than one-fourth of the Caucasian and ethnic minority students who responded to this survey believed at least one of their teachers knew they truanted, they still continued to truant.

TRUANCY AND LANGUAGE SPOKEN AT HOME

Another relationship explored in this study was between truancy and the language spoken at home. We found that 1,542 (63.8%) of the 2,416 students who said they speak English at home admitted to truanting. Spanish was another option the students could choose. Of the 175 students who said they speak Spanish at home, 136 (77.7%) said they truanted. And, of the 136 students who listed another language besides English or Spanish as the language spoken at home, 85 (62.5%) admitted that they truanted.

In addition, class truancy was the preferred type of truancy in all cases: English speakers at home (50.1%), Spanish speakers at home (43.4%), and the "other" language at home category (36.5%). Clearly, we found a higher incidence of overall truancy among the students who speak Spanish at home and class truancy among the participants who speak English at home.

TRUANCY AND THE PERIOD
OF THE DAY MOST OFTEN MISSED

Another purpose of this study was to find out which class period of the day truants were most likely to miss. The question on the survey was "if you cut class, which period of the day do you miss most often? (Please check only one)." The choices were: "first period in the morning," "mid-morning," "last class before lunch," "first class after lunch," "mid-afternoon," and "last period of the day." The students were also given the option to specify that they had "no particular pattern" to their truanting.

The data revealed that "no particular pattern" was selected most often for both Caucasian and ethnic minority students. Next to "no particular pattern," the first period of the day and the last period of the day were preferred for the Caucasian truants. Interestingly, but not surprisingly, the ethnic minority truants preferred the last period of the day followed by the class periods before and after lunch.

These data are consistent with what we would expect. Students perhaps think that these periods are the safest to cut without being caught or are the most convenient to cut by offering the longest chunk of time before being expected back in class.

CONCLUSIONS

The findings from the preceding tables suggest that most students believe education is important and that their parents and friends encourage them to succeed. They also feel that their school has a strict policy on truancy, which is enforced.

We have sufficiently stated why truancy continues to occur at an alarming level. After careful analysis, to suppose that their truanting behavior is motivated by juvenile delinquency is illogical. A more logical explanation is that, while these students know education is important—and that parents and friends support them—a disconnect exists between them and their education, and it is driving them away.

Many parts and courses of education were considered in relation to truancy. The results we have discussed are troubling to say the least. Truancy exists in large part because of reasons involving curriculum, pedagogy, teacher behavior, and other school-related issues. Truants claim that they value education, their parents value education, and their schools have policies in place, yet these same truants purposely absent themselves from the very education they value. Whatever is pulling these truants away from school and class is strong enough to jeopardize the future opportunities and life that only a solid education can provide. Understanding the truancy phenomena and embracing the challenges it is providing will lead us to the conclusion that the real problem is not with our students but with our schools, a message our students are trying to tell us.

Chapter Seven

Truancy among English Language Learners

Truancy is a universal phenomenon: "universal" in the sense that truancy does not happen for groups differentiated by intellectual ability, academic success, grade levels, or social classes. Research now shows that truancy is found among and across different ethnicity groups and among students learning English as a second language.

Many students come to the United States from other countries, on their own or with their families, with very limited English language proficiency. Understandably, their native language continues to be spoken among their family members and friends in their homes and communities. Yet these students must acculturate themselves in the American schools where most of the instruction is done in English.

Research shows that for most people, the younger a person is when the immersion in a second language occurs, the quicker that he or she will become proficient in that language. Hence, many of these foreign students will become proficient in English. However, because not all of them arrive in America at the ideal age for language learning, many will not.

By way of definition, English as a *first* language refers to those students who were raised speaking English. These students may or may not be Caucasian by race, but English is the first language they learned fluently. English as a *second* language (ESL), then, refers to those students who are learning, or have learned, English as a second (or even a third, etc.) language. In our public schools, these students are more commonly referred to as English language learners (ELL), which is the term we use in this book.

An important focus of this book is to explore the relationship between truancy and English language learners. If truancy is related to curriculum and pedagogical factors, as research shows and as we contend, then students who are learning English as a second language might be prone to truancy. Of course, we are not saying that such truancy is inevitable, but the relationship is obvious enough. To substantiate the relationship, we will now turn to a few interesting statistics.

ETHNICITY AND LANGUAGES

As mentioned previously, a major truancy study was done in the western United States (Shute, 2009). Table 7.1 shows the ethnic background of the participants who speak English as a first language or as a second

Table 7.1.   ELL students by race.

	English as a First Language (%)	English as a Second Language (%)	Total (%)
Caucasian	1867 (96.5)	67 (3.5)	1934 (70.9)
Hispanic	180 (49.9)	181 (50.1)	361 (13.2)
Asian	61 (46.2)	71 (53.8)	132 (4.8)
Pacific Islander	60 (68.2)	28 (31.8)	88 (3.2)
African American	43 (76.8)	13 (30.2)	56 (2.1)
Native American	37 (88.1)	5 (11.9)	42 (1.5)
Middle East	8 (61.5)	5 (38.5)	13 (0.5)
Other*	79 (78.2)	22 (21.8)	101 (3.7)
Total	2335 (85.6)	392 (14.4)	2727

*Note. A reminder to the reader is in order regarding the "other" category of ethnicity. The "other" category is comprised of students who not only checked the "other" category as their ethnicity but also students who did not indicate their ethnic background or checked the "other" category and then proceeded to write one of the races already given as their ethnic background.

The data from the "other" category in some instances are deemed inconclusive, but the data for the current topic of language are valid. Of these 101 students, 79 (78.2%) said they speak English as a first language (which is surprising in itself because the survey was written in English) and 22 (21.8%) said they speak English as a second language.

language. The data are organized in descending order from the largest ethnic group surveyed.

A rich collection of ethnic backgrounds showed up in the data, which yielded an interesting mix of ELL students from all ethnic categories. A total of 2,727 participants completed the survey, of whom 392 (14.4%) said they speak English as a second language. The Hispanic students (361) made up the largest group of ethnic minorities, and 181 (50.1%) of them speak English as a second language. Of course, the high percentage of Caucasian students who speak English as their first language is expected, given that the majority of the participants were white Americans.

TRUANCY AND FIRST LANGUAGE

The study on which this research is based revealed that as a group, the students who speak English as a second language had an overall higher incidence of truancy than the students who speak English as a first language (table 7.2). In addition, the data also show that class truancy was preferred by both first and second language speakers. This finding is consistent with all minority groups preferring class truancy.

To understand truancy better, results from the survey categorized truancy into three categories: school truants (truants who only skipped entire days of school), class truants (truants who only skipped classes after they arrived at school), and students who truanted from both class and school. Of the 2,335 total truants who speak English as a first language, 1,488 (63.7%) were truants, and 748 (50.3%) of these truants skipped class only.

Table 7.2. ELL truancy and type of truancy.

	Total (%)	Nontruants (%)	Total Truants (%)	School Truants (%)	Class Truants (%)	Both (%)
English as a	2335	847	1488	271	748	469
First **Language**	(85.6)	(36.3)	(63.7)	(18.2)	(50.3)	(31.5)
English as a	392	117	275	61	114	100
Second **Language**	(14.4)	(29.8)	(70.2)	(22.2)	(41.5)	(36.4)
	2727	964	1763	332	862	569

Of the 392 students who said they speak English as a second language, 275 (70.2%) admitted that they truant, and 114 (41.5%) said they skipped class only. If this high incidence of truancy were a snapshot of truancy nationwide (and research shows that it is), a major challenge exists in servicing these students who are choosing to not attend certain classes throughout the day and are, therefore, not in their seats at school.

In this study, the incidence of class-only truancy was nearly triple that of school-only truancy for students who speak English as a first language and nearly double for students who speak English as a second language.

COMPARING TRUANCY AMONG ELL AND NON-ELL SPEAKERS

If English language learners (ELL) were more likely to truant than English speakers (non-ELL), as data show that they are, we want to know if this difference is significant. In other words, with what level of confidence can we say that the data we found on this particular school day will be consistent with data found on any other school day?

Table 7.3 compares truancy levels between the students who speak English as a first language and students who speak English as a second language.

As shown in table 7.3, the truancy level for the ELL students was 70.2% (SD .46) compared to the lower level of 63.7% for non-ELL students. The t-test shows that these mean differences are significant at the $<.05$ level of confidence (p = .0053). In other words, we can say with a

Table 7.3. Simple statistics for truancy among students regarding ELL as measured by Item 106.

Group	n	Truancy Level	SD
ELL: Yes	392	70.2%	0.46
ELL: No	2335	63.7%	0.48

T-test for comparing hypothesis that ELL students are *more* likely to truant than non-ELL students.

Test for ELL Students	T-Stat	P-Value
ELL truancy greater than non-ELL truancy	2.55	.0053*

* Indicates significance at or beyond <0.05.

significant level of confidence that ELL students are more likely to truant than non-ELL students.

TRUANCY BY RACE AND ENGLISH
AS A FIRST OR SECOND LANGUAGE

Another interesting aspect of truancy is comparing the ethnic background of the truants who speak English as a second language to those who speak English as a first language from the same ethnic background; for example, comparing Hispanics who speak English as a first language to Hispanics who speak English as a second language. Table 7.4 shows this comparison.

The data show that of the 1,934 Caucasian students, 1,897 speak English as a first language and 67 speak English as a second language. This wide gap was to be expected since most Caucasians in the area where

Table 7.4.   English as a second language truancy compared to English as a first language truancy.

	Total Students	English as a First Language Students	English as a First Language Truants (%)	English as a Second Language Students	English as a Second Language Truants (%)
Caucasian	1934	1897	1155 (60.9)	67	49 (73.1)
Minority Groups*	692	389	284 (73.0)	304	210 (69.1)
Hispanic	361	180	145 (80.6)	181	134 (74.0)
African American	56	43	31 (72.1)	13	10 (76.9)
Asian	132	61	33 (54.1)	71	43 (60.6)
Native American	42	37	28 (75.7)	5	3 (60.0)
Pacific Islander	88	60	43 (71.7)	29	16 (55.2)
Middle East	13	8	4 (50.0)	5	4 (80.0)
Other	101	79	49 (62.0)	22	16 (72.7)

* Does not include the "other" category.

the survey was administered were white Americans. Of the Caucasian students who speak English as a first language, 1,155 (60.9%) said they truanted. Of the 67 Caucasian students who speak English as a second language, 49 (73.1%) were truants.

A much higher percentage was found among those Caucasian truants who speak English as a second language than those who speak English as a first language. This trend was not true for the ethnic minority students in this study.

Of the 692 ethnic minority students, 389 speak English as a first language and 304 speak English as a second language. Of these 389 ethnic minority students who speak English as a first language, 284 (73.0%) said they truanted. However, of the 304 ethnic minority students who speak English as a second language, 210 (69.1%) said they truanted.

In this case, the percentage of ethnic minority truants who speak English as a second language is less than the percentage of ethnic minority truants who speak English as a first language. Although the gap is not as wide as for the Caucasian students, it is clear that a gap exists. This overall percentage for the ethnic minority students was taken from the specific ethnic minority groups represented in this study.

Specifically, of the 361 Hispanic students in this study, 180 speak English as a first language and 181 speak English as a second language. Of these 180 Hispanic students who speak English as a first language, 145 (80.6%) said they truanted. At the same time, of the 181 Hispanic students who speak English as a second language, 134 (74.0%) said they truanted. Of the 132 Asian students who participated in the study, 61 speak English as a first language and 71 speak English as a second language. Of these 61 students who speak English as a first language, 33 (54.1%) said they truanted. On the other hand, of the 71 Asian students who speak English as a second language, 43 (60.6%) said they truanted. The number of students in the other ethnic categories was relatively small for research purposes. However, the results can still be useful.

The students from the African American and Asian ethnic groups who speak English as a second language joined the Caucasian group who had a higher incidence of truancy than their peers who speak English as a first language. The opposite was true with the Hispanic students. They had a higher incidence of truancy among the students who speak English as a first language.

ENGLISH LANGUAGE LEARNERS
AND FREQUENCY OF TRUANCY

In addition to the incidence of truancy, the frequency with which these students truant is also important. The participants indicated how often they had truanted in the two months prior to completing the survey. The students were asked to indicate if they truanted "not very often (e.g., 1–2 *days* or 1–2 *classes*)," "often (e.g., 1 *day* a week or 1–2 *classes* a week)," or "very often (e.g., 2 or more *days* a week or 2 or more *classes* a week)." Table 7.5 shows the data from their responses.

The data show that the overwhelming majority of truancy is occurring "not very often" among both the students who speak English as a first language (77.2%) and students who speak English as a second language (71.6%). This means that the majority of students pick and choose which classes they truant from and did so at least 1–2 entire days of school or 1–2 classes in the previous two months before completing the survey.

Individually, this does not seem like much. However, combining the groups of English as a first language and English as a second language speakers, this is 1,346 students missing one (1,346) student days/classes or two (2,692) student days/classes over approximately 40 school days (two months). We must ask ourselves if this is acceptable.

Furthermore, while we consider the amount of classes missed by these students, we cannot ignore the students who truant "often" and "very often." These students are truanting at least one day or one/two classes *a week*. The lost learning for all of these truants is remarkable— especially, as we consider the students who are learning English as a second language. The more school they miss, the less English learning they gain.

Table 7.5. Frequency of truancy among ELL students.

	Total (%)	Nontruants (%)	Total Truants (%)	Not Very Often (%)	Often (%)	Very Often (%)
English as a *First* **Language**	2335 (85.6)	847 (36.3)	1488 (63.7)	1149 (77.2)	233 (15.7)	106 (7.1)
English as a *Second* **Language**	392 (14.4)	117 (29.8)	275 (70.2)	197 (71.6)	43 (15.6)	35 (12.7)
	2727	964	1763	1346	276	141

Without doubt, these students will learn some English being in the United States, whether or not they are physically present in school; but to succeed academically, the importance of being in school is hardly arguable. Thus truancy leads to lost English proficiency, which in turn leads to an unsuccessful school/class experience, which is followed by more truancy.

SPEAKERS OF ENGLISH AS A SECOND LANGUAGE AND PROFICIENCY LEVELS

Once the number of students who speak English as a second language was identified, the survey elicited from these students their self-determined level of English proficiency to determine if their English proficiency level played a role in their truancy behavior. Since the students who classified themselves as English language learners (ELL) were not given an English proficiency test, we asked these students to make a self-assessment as to their proficiency level in four categories of English: understanding, reading, writing, and speaking.

UNDERSTANDING ENGLISH PROFICIENCY

The first distinction the survey made was as to how well these English language learners *understand* English. In other words, how would they rate their level of English comprehension? The students were asked to what degree they agreed with the statement "I understand English well."

The data show that those students who stated that they understand English well were much more likely *not* to truant than those who stated that they did not understand English well. Of the 275 ELL truants, 43 (15.6%) strongly disagreed, somewhat disagreed, or were neutral concerning the statement. Of the 117 ELL nontruants, only 7 (5.9%) were neutral. None of the ELL nontruants strongly disagreed or disagreed with the statement.

In other words, of the 50 total students who strongly disagreed, disagreed, or were neutral, 43 (86.0%) were truants. Interestingly, none of the 117 ELL nontruants disagreed or strongly disagreed with this statement, but 20 of the ELL truants did. This suggests that a perception of

Table 7.6. Simple statistics for truancy among ELL students regarding their proficiency at understanding English as measured by Item 107.

Group	n	Mean Score	SD
ELL Truants	275	4.4	1.09
ELL Nontruants	117	4.7	0.57

T-test for comparing hypothesis that ELL students who claim lower proficiency in understanding English are *more* likely to truant than those who claim higher proficiency.

Test for ELL Students with Understanding English	T-Stat	P-Value
Regarding understanding English: lower proficiency ELL students greater than higher proficiency ELL students	−3.52	.0002*

* Indicates significance at or beyond <0.05.

not understanding English well would be a cause of truancy, although it would only identify about 7.4% of all truants.

We can clearly see, however, that the majority of ELL truants and nontruants said they understand English well. Over 84.0% of the 275 truants claimed that they understand English well. For these students, their truancy is based on some other aspect of their educational day.

Using the students' level of agreement on the five-point Likert scale to the statement "I understand English well," we were able to apply a t-test for the comparison. Table 7.6 shows the results when a t-test was applied.

The table shows that a significant difference exists (p = .0002), with means of 4.4 (SD 1.09) for ELL truants versus 4.7 (SD 0.57) for the nontruants. Thus, while both groups had learned English as a second language, those who claimed that they "understood" English better were less likely to be truant.

WRITING ENGLISH PROFICIENCY

The next statement these ELL students responded to was "I write English well enough to do my schoolwork properly." This statement differentiated from the previous question by focusing on the student's English writing ability as opposed to their ability to understand English.

A large portion of a day at school is presumably spent writing and, therefore, may be a hindrance to some students who believe that they do not write well, especially those who are in the process of learning English as a second language, and perhaps already have a low confidence level with the language.

Students who speak English as a second language and believe that they do not write well were much more likely to truant than those who believe that they do write well. Of the 274 ELL truants who responded to this statement, 55 (20.1%) strongly disagreed, somewhat disagreed, or were neutral concerning the statement. Of the 117 ELL nontruants, only 12 (10.3%) were neutral.

In other words, of the 67 total students who strongly disagreed, disagreed, or were neutral, 55 (82.1%) were truants. Interestingly, none of the 117 ELL nontruants strongly disagreed or disagreed with this statement, but 25 of the ELL truants did. This suggests that a perception of not writing English well would be a cause of truancy.

Using the students' level of agreement on the five-point Likert scale to the statement "I write English well enough to do my school work properly," we were able to apply a t-test for the comparison. Table 7.7 shows the results when a t-test was applied, and, again, a significant difference existed between ELL truants and ELL nontruants.

As shown in table 7.7, the mean score for the ELL truants was 4.3 (SD 1.14), and it was 4.6 (SD .67) for the ELL nontruants. The t-test shows that this is a significant difference ($p = .0024$). Students who are learning English as a second language and who rate themselves as poorer at

Table 7.7. Simple statistics for truancy among ELL students regarding their proficiency at writing English as measured by Item 108.

Group	n	Mean Score	STD
ELL Truants	274	4.3	1.14
ELL Nontruants	117	4.6	0.67

T-test for comparing hypothesis that ELL students who claim lower proficiency in writing English truant *more* than those who claim higher proficiency.

Test for ELL Students with English Writing Proficiency	T-Stat	P-Value
Regarding writing English: lower proficiency ELL students greater than higher proficiency ELL students	−2.83	.0024*

* Indicates significance at or beyond <0.05.

English writing proficiency than other ELL students are more likely to truant. However, the majority of English language learners believed that they write well enough to do their schoolwork proficiently, including the truants, and therefore must be truanting for other reasons.

READING ENGLISH PROFICIENCY

The next statement the students responded to was "I read English well enough to understand my school work properly." This statement differentiated from the previous two in that it focuses on reading ability. Good proficiency in reading, like in writing, is an incredibly important skill for a student to be successful in his or her studies.

Students who speak English as a second language and stated that they do not read English well enough to understand their schoolwork properly were more likely to truant than those who claimed that they do read well enough to understand their schoolwork. Of the 275 students who responded to this statement, 55 (20.0%) strongly disagreed, somewhat disagreed, or were neutral regarding this statement. Of the 117 ELL nontruants, 10 (8.5%) claimed that they disagreed or were neutral.

In total, of the 65 students who strongly disagreed, disagreed, or were neutral (meaning that they do not read English well enough to be successful), 55 (84.6%) of them were truants. Again, as with understanding and writing English, this finding suggests that a perception of not reading English well would be an indicator of truancy.

Most of the students indicated that they read English well enough to understand their schoolwork properly. Using the students' level of agreement on the five-point Likert scale to the statement "I read English well enough to understand my schoolwork properly," we were able to apply a t-test for the comparison. Table 7.8 shows the results when a t-test was applied. A significant difference also appears for this item.

The mean score of the ELL truants' responses was 4.4 (SD 1.12) while the mean score of the ELL nontruants' responses was 4.6 (SD .76). Even though these mean scores are very close, we found that the difference is significant ($p = .0041$). The t-test result shows that the truancy level of ELL students who perceive their English reading proficiency to be low

Table 7.8. Simple statistics for truancy among ELL students regarding their proficiency at reading English as measured by Item 109.

Group	n	Mean Score	SD
ELL Truants	275	4.4	1.12
ELL Nontruants	117	4.6	0.76

T-test for comparing hypothesis that ELL students who claim lower proficiency in reading English truant *more* than those who claim higher proficiency.

Test for ELL Students with English Reading Proficiency	T-Stat	P-Value
Regarding reading English: lower proficiency ELL students greater than higher proficiency ELL students	−2.66	.0041*

*Indicates significance at or beyond <0.05.

is significantly different from those who perceive their English reading proficiency to be high. Poor English reading proficiency would be an indicator related to truancy.

SPEAKING ENGLISH PROFICIENCY

The final statement in this section of the survey was "I speak English well enough to communicate with others at school." Interestingly, many students who are learning English as a second language believe that they can read, write, and understand English well, but truants and nontruants alike stated that they have trouble speaking it.

Statistically, not speaking English well enough to communicate with others is still a strong cause of truancy. Of the 275 truants, 46 (16.7%) strongly disagreed, somewhat disagreed, or were neutral. In addition, of the 116 nontruants who responded to the survey, 7 (6.0%) strongly disagreed, somewhat disagreed, or were neutral.

Interestingly, the 18 (6.5%) ELL truants who strongly disagreed, meaning that they do not believe they speak English well enough to communicate in English with others at school, represent the highest percentage in the "strongly disagree" category for each of the statements regarding reading, writing, and understanding English in this section of the survey. This means that more of these ELL truants believe their English speaking ability is their biggest roadblock to doing well in school and thus attending.

Table 7.9. Simple statistics for truancy among ELL students regarding their proficiency at speaking English.

Group	n	Mean Score	SD
ELL Truants	275	4.4	1.14
ELL Nontruants	116	4.7	0.70

T-test for comparing hypothesis that ELL students who claim lower proficiency in speaking English truant *more* than those who claim higher proficiency.

Test for ELL Students with Perceived English Speaking Proficiency	T-Stat	P-Value
Regarding speaking English: lower proficiency ELL students greater than higher proficiency ELL students	−3.21	.0007*

* Indicates significance at or beyond <0.05.

Again, using the students' level of agreement on the five-point Likert scale to the statement "I speak English well enough to communicate with others at school," we were able to apply a t-test for the comparison. Table 7.9 shows the results. A significant difference also appears for this item.

The mean score was 4.4 (SD 1.14) for the ELL truants and 4.7 (SD .70) for the ELL nontruants. The t-stat is −3.21 and is highly significant beyond the <.05 level (p = .0007). This shows that a perceived speaking proficiency is a strong predictor of truancy.

Asking the ELL students to rate themselves in English proficiency and analyzing that data proved to be very insightful. A highly significant difference appeared for all four areas of English proficiency. The scope of this research was not to accurately measure the students' English proficiency with a language test; however, it is clear that a significant difference exists in the truancy level among ELL students who perceive their English language proficiency to be low compared to ELL students who perceive their English language proficiency to be high. In light of the significant difference discovered, language proficiency is an issue that needs attention.

By way of caution, we understand that inherent in any survey written in English and administered to students who are proficient in English at varying degrees of proficiency lends itself to the possibility for uncertain responses. Students who are learning English as a second language may not adequately understand the survey items written in English due to their lower English proficiency level. However, this does not render their responses of no value.

Analysis shows that students who perceived their proficiency to be low in understanding, reading, writing, and speaking English were more likely to truant. We are not saying that these students are doomed to truancy. We are saying that the difference in perceived English language proficiency between truants and nontruants who speak English as a second language was significant.

REFERENCE

Shute, J. W. (2009). *Expanding the truancy debate: Truancy, ethnic minorities and English language learners*. In M. Conolly and D. O'Keeffe (Eds.), *Don't Fence Me In: Essays on the Rational Truant* (pp. 115–38). Buckingham, England: The University of Buckingham Press.

Chapter Eight

Shifting the Prevailing Winds of Education

The joy of teaching and learning is immeasurable. However, in the evolution of our education system, the joy of teaching and learning is being replaced by pressure. This pressure comes from more and more high-stakes testing, longer days and hours, and more federal mandates, policies, and requirements, which all take away the positive quality of our teaching and learning.

Many administrators, teachers, parents, and students are disappointed in the education provided by our learning institutions and are increasingly and rapidly losing confidence in them as well. Disappointment may not be the conscious choice of words they would use, but surely the emotion is felt. For decades, this disappointment and loss of confidence have brought a call from all parts and groups of society for changes in our education system.

Truancy is a specific indication of how well our education system is doing. As has been shown, the incidence and frequency of truancy are staggering. Should the education establishment continue to claim that 70–90% of our students are juvenile delinquents who truant because of psychological or social problems? This is, in fact, what we are claiming, if we continue to lay blame for truancy at the feet of the truants and society.

We stated earlier in this book that we strongly disagree with this notion. Our assertion is that while we agree that some truants fit this profile, most truants are rational decision-makers choosing to truant to escape the classroom and what is happening there.

We acknowledge that in making this claim, we may offend some teachers, which is not our intent. Our specific intention here is to promote another more rational view of truancy, a view that, if pursued, will lessen the truancy problem. This view is that many truants are avoiding school and class as a rational choice because the teaching and pedagogy are not fulfilling expectations.

Thoughtful, well-meaning teachers put untold hours of time and energy into the development of our nation's youth. These devoted teachers and educators are true heroes whom our youth continue to need, but whom our education system continues to devalue.

State education departments and school administrators do not like truancy for obvious reasons: namely, money. Funding for schools is determined by enrollment. If students are absent, enrollment is lower and funding is less. However, another, perhaps more subtle, reason is that truancy exposes the weaknesses of schools.

Only a few states are willing to make their truancy data public or let truancy research take place. We understand. If truancy surfaced as a serious institutional problem, it may be attributed to school officials. Most researchers who have studied truancy have experienced this resistance.

A personal story illustrates this resistance and the typical response by some educational elites. When trying to administer a survey for truancy research in a Western state, some administrators informed us that conducting our research in this area was nothing short of illegal. They cited the "Federal Educational Rights and Privacy Act" (FERPA), which protects minors from being incriminated by answering questions about their own illegal behavior. Since truancy is illegal because of compulsory schooling laws in the United States, administrators cannot have minors respond to a survey about it.

We countered that provisions must be put in place for these kinds of surveys since many studies on student illegal behavior, including drug and alcohol abuse, abound. We then discovered, without the help of these administrators, that many federal laws are appended in some states. After carefully examining this federal statute, we discovered that a provision for administering anonymous surveys exists if the data could not and would not be linked to either the particular students or the schools they were attending.

After finding this provision, we approached the school district a second time only to be informed that while the *federal* statute does allow for anonymous surveys of this type, the *state's* modification of that statute did not. Our appeals ultimately ended with the governor of the state and hence the chief counsel of the State Board of Education, who confirmed those limitations.

We approached other school districts in the same state with interesting results. Some districts informed us that while truancy research is a worthy cause, the time it would take and the intrusion into the classroom did not warrant the effort. In addition, fear of litigation by parents of students was cited as the secondary reason for the denied access to students for this research.

We were also told that the school district already knew that the problem of truancy exists and that they did not need a study to inform them of it. Of course, this type of reasoning is the antithesis of education. Isn't education supposed to be for learning how to solve problems, to become better people? Apparently, hypocrisy thrives in some school settings. The open floodgate of problems appears to be drowning administrators in education, and truancy is just another problem they haphazardly deal with as they try to stay afloat.

Eventually, we found a local school board that was excited about our research because it would help them to better understand which classes students enjoyed and which classes they didn't. Apparently, at the time businesses in the area were pressuring schools to offer classes that would better prepare our young people for entrance into, and success in, a competitive global marketplace. Interestingly, the education establishment was fighting these efforts vigorously in favor of a more "balanced" liberal arts education.

After we were cleared to administer the survey in different schools, we found that principals were also divided on the topic of truancy. Fortunately, the principal of a large high school openly acknowledged a truancy problem and wanted to find out whether recently implemented truancy policies were having a positive effect on the problem. She was also interested in how the students perceived the school and the problem of truancy itself.

She went out of her way to accommodate our requests and became more actively involved as the project progressed. On the day of the survey, she took upon herself the leadership, which allowed our research team to take a supportive role to her and the other school administrators.

Since we eventually were able to carry out our research, the legal reasons, and other issues noted previously for not allowing our research, appear to be a smokescreen to cover up a deeper issue. The question must be asked: If those schools are seriously deficient, would it not be in the public interest to identify and correct the deficiencies? How else might it be done?

As educators, we understand that time in the classroom is precious. Papers to grade, lesson plans to make and review, classroom management issues to attend to, and a host of other jobs to be done—all of which lead to tension when someone wants to intrude into a school day with a survey.

However, this open opposition has been a cause of concern. Why is there an apparent resentment to finding solutions to big problems in the educational system of our country? Won't solutions help our students achieve more? In a very literal sense, we must ask: is *equality* the goal, or is *excellence* the goal? The idea that we can achieve excellence, regardless of federal programs and initiatives that claim we can, is fading away. We are increasingly becoming content with equality, always searching for programs that cater to mediocrity. The magic wand of excellence is hard work.

Reports abound regarding the achievement levels of the pupils in our schools. One such report states that one-third of our first-year college students read below a seventh-grade level, and "America's public schools graduate 700,000 functionally illiterate kids every year, while 700,000 more drop out. Four out of five young adults in a recent survey couldn't summarize the main point of a newspaper article, read a bus schedule, or figure their change from a restaurant bill" (Murphy, 1990, pp. 11–18).

As the educational system declines, the cries that America's leadership is at risk are heard. Robert J. Herbold, a member of the President's Council of Advisors on Science and Technology, in an article titled "K–12 Establishment is Putting America's Industrial Leadership at Risk," states, "There are some very worrisome trends in the United States with respect to our global share of science, technology, engineering and mathematics expertise" (2005, p. 1).

The trends are spiraling downward. In 2001 the United States ranked last among Singapore, Germany, China, South Korea, Taiwan, the United Kingdom, Sweden, and Belgium in engineering and science degrees as a percentage of all bachelor degrees, with China producing three times more engineers than the United States.

Herbold further states that over 50% of the CEOs of our Fortune 100 companies come from technical backgrounds. According to Herbold, since the number of our science and technology graduates is declining while at the same time rising in other parts of the world, our industrial leadership is weakening (2005, p. 1).

Herbold claims that the main reason for this deterioration and the poor performance we see in school is that we have a weak curriculum and unqualified teachers, both of which contribute to truancy. The statistics show that an alarming 81% of our twelfth graders are at a "partial proficient or below partial proficiency" level, while only 2% are "advanced" and 16% are "Proficient" (2005, p. 2). The statistics for our fourth and eighth graders are similarly bleak. The statistics show that only 30% of the students who enter a science track in ninth grade are still interested in science upon entering college (p. 4).

We can agree with Herbold's criticisms without sharing his motives. Our job is to educate, not necessarily to train an economically competitive labor force. If there were a simple relationship between successful numbers of engineers and mathematicians, then Communism would have won the battle for world supremacy many years ago, since the Communists have produced countless engineers. The problem is not that we are *not* producing enough engineers and scientists, but we are producing too many illiterate and innumerate ones.

In addition to being one of the most neglected topics in the sociology of education, truancy reflects the central problem of mass education in free societies—its institutionalization of the education elite's mindset and its neglect of popular preferences. The adversarial conflicts of politicians have infiltrated the education system. Now, without any attempt to consult parents, students, or consumers, we find strange ideas and notions taking over the classroom.

The purposes of education were once agreed upon as the achievement of literacy, numeracy, familiarity with the American culture, and a sense of moral conscience for the better good of society—to become better people. Views of education were not severely divided; the elite and the commoner saw education as striving to reach the same goals.

In the recent past, beginning in the 1950s, the education system has been "dumbed" down in the name of progress, liberating young minds, and producing free thinkers. The side effects of these notions are now quite apparent. Students' handwriting is atrocious, illiteracy abounds, many pupils cannot spell correctly, and, yes, test scores are still low and declining.

Truancy data constitute incomparably rich policy material. We already know that semi-literates truant because they cannot do the work, and clever children truant because the work is derisory. We know that a minority of students dislike physical education. We know foreign languages are usually poorly taught in America. We know that wrong methods of teaching reading have been practiced for years in America and Britain for almost a century. In both countries, mathematics teaching is appalling. In both systems, political correctness has raged through the curriculum, destroying the authority of the teachers.

Because of public financing, and because of the dominance of an elite stratum, schools have developed an alternative agenda, a suboptimal curriculum and pedagogy different from what the citizens would have chosen if they were asked. The goal of education is to learn, to grow. But the administrators who have control are closed-minded to learning and growing. "If we are truly committed to transforming our public schools from the underclass factories they have become into an effective system of universal public education, we must allow ourselves to be guided by reason and evidence" (Coulsen, 2004, p. 3).

VIEWS OF EDUCATION

A recent newspaper article proclaims, "Gates says U.S. high schools ripe for reform." The article expresses how Microsoft Corp. Chairman Bill Gates opened the latest National Education Summit where the nation's governors united to vent their frustrations on the state of America's high schools. The article states that Gates told "the nation's governors and leaders of the educational community that the nation's high schools are obsolete and need radical restructuring to raise graduation rates, prepare students for college and train a workforce that faces growing competition in the global economy." Gates goes on to say that "our high schools were designed 50 years ago to meet the needs of another age. Until we design them to meet the needs of this century, we will keep limiting, even ruining, the lives of millions of Americans every year" (Balz, 2005, p. 11A).

Again, the poor intellectual quality of many students demands educational reform. Truancy does not happen because students know they are going to end up in rotten jobs but because they are unstimulated and unfulfilled intellectually by bad curriculum and bad teaching.

The summit also highlighted the dropout problems and the "schools' failure to give students adequate preparation for college and to developing an agenda for action in the states." This summit is sponsored by the National Governors Association and Achieve Inc., a partnership created by the governors and the business community to increase standards and accountability in education. The decline of our education system "threatens the United States as the preeminent economic power in the world." Among the alarming statistics that Gates enumerated were that "the United States ranks 16th among 20 developed nations in the percentage of students who complete high school and 14th among the top 20 in college graduation rates. Just 18 of 100 students entering high school go on to complete their college degree within six years of starting college. America has slipped from first to fifth internationally in the percentage of young people who hold a college degree" (Balz, 2005, p. 11A).

Yet, despite these calls to reform by people like Gates, who are outside the education field, administrators in the education field continue to prevent a better set of practices from emerging by not facilitating, allowing, and acknowledging research.

While the ideas addressed have promise, they have been said many times before. The reason that no changes are made is not because the ideas are too grandiose but because at the heart of the problem is a distorted perspective on what education should be about.

PROBLEM OF METAPHOR

In discussing the problems the education system in our country is facing, Shute contends that truancy, as well as dropout rates, low achievement, and other ailments that plague teachers and administrators, are symptoms of the problem, not the problem itself (Shute, 1994, p. 1). Administrators, legislators, school board members, and educators continue searching for better programs: programs that are essentially trying to put a bandage on the wounds while the root of the illness is ignored.

All teachers and administrators, like all other human beings, carry around with them metaphors, and they bring their metaphors into the daily operation of school. Teachers conduct their classrooms and administrators run their schools according to the metaphors they have adopted.

A metaphor is a comparison between two things on the basis of a similarity that exists between them. Metaphors shape our point of view of all things and ultimately our behaviors, whether we are aware of their presence or not. For example, think of the way a man might view his role as a father. Is he a boss? A coach? A pal? A bystander? Or is he some combination of these or other things? *Something* inside of him propels him to act a certain way as a father, and that something is the *metaphor*—the way he sees his role.

At the root of our education problem is a faulty fundamental metaphor, or lens, through which we view the purpose of education and act in our classrooms. We may think that, as educators, we all share a common goal for our students—learning. But what is the goal of learning? And how best do we achieve this goal? How do we know that we have achieved this goal?

For example, working these three questions backward, we observe that the only way we seem to be able to know whether our children have achieved the goal of learning is by giving them a test, which means the best way to achieve the goal of learning is to prepare them for the test, which means our goal is to put enough "knowledge" in their heads so that they can successfully pass the test.

Tragically, because of programs such as No Child Left Behind (NCLB), imposed without mindful practice of sound learning and teaching principles, "classroom instruction has been transformed into test preparation." Many studies have shown that this has occurred "since the implementation of NCLB, rigid curriculum objectives and mechanistic preparation for state standardized testing hijacked curricular diversity and pedagogical exploration and flexibility" (Zhao, 2012, p. 40).

Unfortunately, the Common Core Standards, the most recent federal program for change, leads to the same test—and its high-stakes results. Well-intentioned administrators and teachers continue to scramble for the best, most effective strategies.

PREVAILING METAPHORS

The most dominant and widely held metaphor of education in the west "is the supplying of a dynamic labor force for the economy" (Shute, 1994, p. 20). In other words, we have educational institutions in our country for the purpose of producing people who can boost production and therefore the economy. Why else do we educate children, if not for them to "get a good job" or to "prepare them for society"? This, of course, worked great in the 19th and 20th centuries, when factories and manufacturing were building our industrialized nation.

"Traditional education," which sees a teacher in front of the class "transferring knowledge" to students obediently sitting in neat rows, was the answer. Students dutifully wondered what they needed to do to "get a good grade."

When students graduated and became employed, they dutifully wondered what they needed to do to get paid, good health benefits, and vacation time. We are now in a world of globalization. For the past 100 years, our schools have been preparing students' mindsets for jobs that rarely exist now, but we continue preparing them.

For a wonderful treatment on the subject of what our students need to compete in a global market and thrive in a digital world, see Yong Zhao's book *World Class Learners* referenced herein. In short, our metaphor of teaching must change if education is to change and we are to prepare successful students for globalization.

Another dominant metaphor in education is that of the assembly line at a bottle factory. Imagine children (the bottles) progressing along a conveyor belt as well-meaning teachers (the workers) pour in small bits and pieces of knowledge, a little here, a little there, until eventually, hopefully after twelve years, we put a cap (graduation) on their heads and proudly proclaim them full of enough knowledge to contribute to society.

This metaphor is manifested in the traditional classroom that now consists of cooperative learning groups of students and teachers who have moved away from the front of the classroom to mingle among his/her students. However, regardless of the class configuration or where the teacher physically stands, isn't this still a bottling factory? The teacher is the "dispenser" of knowledge, with different strategies on how to dispense it.

The final metaphor that is treated in this book is the metaphor of the student's mind being a computer. Of course, a computer is perfect for what it does, storing enormous amounts of information and data and then recalling those data instantly. In this metaphor, we see a teacher who has the knowledge, and he/she inputs it into the student's brain using one technique or another.

The student is required to store the data and retrieve it whenever called upon, whether in discussion or on a test. The teacher becomes a technician, inputting information into the child's "computer," who then should be able to recall the data instantly. Schools and teachers are judged by whether or not the student can adequately recall the information. Learning is all about data entry, and teaching then becomes *not* about meaning but about techniques and strategies to achieve the best test results.

To understand why this is an incorrect metaphor, we must understand the *difference* between the mind and the computer. The human mind can do things the computer cannot do and will never be able to do. A human mind can think, imagine, weigh, ponder, wonder, and judge. The mind, thankfully, has the power to consider things, to think about life, with all its ironies and paradoxes, with all its perplexities and problems, and from it search for meaning.

The problem with these metaphors, of course, is that human beings are not bottles on a conveyor belt, and they are not computers. We are, after all, human beings. These faulty metaphors are not compatible with the human condition; rather, they are the very antithesis of what we are as human beings.

As mentioned earlier, the underlying problem with these faulty educational metaphors is that they do not foster wonder, skepticism, inspiration, faith, and reflection. These metaphors do not "aim to develop wonder and doubt but mere expertise, reproducible and automatic. [They] do not help individuals to be capable of skepticism and reflection but turn out 'graduates' who are performers for designated tasks and specific operations—possessors only of skills" (Shute, 1994, p. 7).

Solway explains, "Granted, we must all be raised to a job or a profession, but education is surely meant to encompass more than preparation for a trade, no matter how complex or abstruse that may be" (quoted in Shute, 1994, pp. 10–11).

Solway continues that such a metaphor is the development of techniques that maximizes classroom efficiency where education becomes training, where knowledge is conceived as something "measurable or quantifiable, that memory is considered as storage and learning as data retrieval, and ultimately, the human spirit as a complicated system of mechanical and electronic functions" (quoted in Shute, 1994, p. 9). And therein lies the problem of modern educational arrangements.

If we buy into these faulty metaphors, then our goal is to discover the strategies, methods, techniques, and programs that help input knowledge efficiently. The end goal then is the input of knowledge, *not* pondering, inquiring, thinking, weighing, and wondering—after all, there isn't enough time according to the way school is presently structured.

When these metaphors dominate our classrooms, teachers are propelled to find the right strategies and techniques with which to disseminate knowledge. In essence, the techniques and strategies become the focus, and soon teaching techniques and strategies by the hundreds infiltrate our classrooms, diverting away the construction of a framework that leads to real meaningful learning, understanding, and intelligence.

Shute contends that the ways we conceive our personal goals for learning, and how best to achieve these goals, and how we determine if our goals are met, are driven by the metaphor we carry around in our minds (1994, p. 1). As a result, very slow progress is made in education as a whole, "because change can only occur when the beliefs and metaphors that form the underpinnings of that system are examined and updated" (Yero, 2010, p. 121).

Until the metaphor changes, the end goal will be the same, and the way we achieve the goal will be the same, regardless of the new program trending now. No program, strategy, or federal mandate will improve education without a different metaphor. In other words, the education reforms in this country that are usually imposed on teachers "do not reflect mindful practices or systems of thinking. Reformers ignore research about learning in favor of statistics about test scores" (Yero, 2010, p. 121).

Of course, many better metaphors of learning and teaching exist in the hearts and minds of teachers. Consider how changing a thought changes the metaphor. Many of us have heard that "life is a journey." We may very well view learning and teaching as a possible journey—but what kind of journey?

Mostly, this journey is a journey across a predetermined landscape. This journey manifests itself when we refer to the material we need to "cover," meaning that the journey is along a "fixed, two-dimensional road. This teacher defines her role in terms of covering a specific distance along that road in a specific amount of time. . . . Notice how the metaphor puts the subject matter—the road to be covered—in the foreground and assigns value to the students with respect to how much of that road they have traversed" (Yero, 2010, p. 55).

Here are some possible phrases we might hear or say: "He's kind of a slow starter, they get behind, she was slowly plowing through it, I hate going over that two or three times, these kids need a push in every direction, if he's lost, he's just going to get further behind, we didn't get to that today . . ." (Yero, 2010, p. 55). Or, "we have a lot to cover today," "stay with me," "quit horse-playing; you will get behind," "if we make it to there, we can go to recess early."

Many teachers think of the concepts and principles they teach—the bits of human wisdom considered "essential knowledge"—as ends in themselves. This adds yet another layer to the *knowledge is a landscape* and *learning is a journey* across that landscape metaphor. *Concepts and principles are objects* that reside at various locations on the knowledge landscape. As students move across the knowledge landscape, they must *pick up* the concepts until they have *covered* it all and arrived at their final destination—Testland. Here teachers make sure that students *possess* the knowledge objects acquired during the journey. . . . As one looks at a student's life in school, it is as if they were on a years-long *scavenger hunt*—moving quickly from place to place and collecting a pre-specified list of treasures. . . . The underlying belief is that the more knowledge objects students possess, the more they have learned. (Yero, 2010, pp. 55–57; original italics)

This metaphor can be changed with a simple thought. What if the journey becomes a journey of *discovery*? Students would then interact with their environment.

In a discovery-oriented interpretation of the metaphor, the teacher and students travel more or less together, along a loosely defined route toward that same destination. But they make frequent stops along the way as students notice something of interest that they wish to explore. There are occasional side trips to unexpected places. At times, groups pursue different paths and, after returning to the main road, report to the class about what they have found. In this interpretation, learning is still a journey, but a very different type of journey. Compare the two interpretations with an around-the-world trip. The first is like a two-week flight . . . cramming in as many sights as you can in your limited time. When you return from the trip, about all you can say about those sights is that you saw them.

The second is an around-the-world cruise, stopping at interesting ports of call and returning to the ship only when you have explored to your heart's content. (Yero, 2010, p. 57)

Many of us have just rolled our eyes, wondering if we have noticed, lately, the curriculum and standards that teachers must use—no time for journeys of discovery. We have noticed. Our goal is to consider, ponder, and ask "if coverage of the knowledge landscape, the collection of pre-defined knowledge objects, and verification of that collection in Testland are the most efficient or effective metaphors in which to characterize and insure student learning" (Yero, 2010, pp. 57–58).

We do not think so. With better metaphors propelling us, our teaching and learning will improve. For a brilliant, comprehensive treatment of metaphors and our education system, see Judith Lloyd Yero's *Teaching in Mind: How Teacher Thinking Shapes Education*, referenced herein.

We recently discovered another metaphor of teaching and learning, which helps us in our journey of discovery. Dr. Teresia K. Teaiwa of Victoria University of Wellington in New Zealand asks us to consider a voyage of the great seafaring canoes. In the not-so-distant past, people of Oceania explored thousands of miles of ocean in canoes. These were large, double-hulled canoes.

Because the Pacific Ocean is as deep, wide and diverse as it is, those Pacific societies that continue to depend most on the ocean for livelihood and identity have tended to develop the arts of navigation and voyaging to remarkable levels of intellectual and spiritual refinement. In fact, in the Micronesian society of Polowat, an appropriately trained and disciplined navigator is considered *pwo*, the most refined and complete man or person in the community. To be ordained as *pwo*, a navigator would have undergone decades of study and practice. This would be made all the more challenging by the absolute eschewal of modern instruments of navigation and a dependence on an understanding of the patterns of the stars, the habits of birds, the significance of clouds, attention to sea swells, sensitivity to the wind. . . . Navigating the greatest ocean in the world requires mastery, because each journey is a temptation of fate—each expedition potentially a voyage towards death. Navigation, ocean going and the business of the pwo, then, are life and death matters, and as such demand nothing less than mastery. (Teaiwa, 2011, p. 218)

Therefore, on board this double-hulled voyage of discovery are individuals with different roles, each paramount to the success of the voyage. The teacher may be the "navigator lying on the bow to better assess the vicissitudes of the wind and ocean currents" (Teaiwa, 2011, p. 215). The canoe also requires a coxswain who steers and a crew with assigned tasks, all vitally important for life and success. These wayfarers must be mutually committed, cooperating and communicating as they sail away from their familiar island out into the open sea of the unknown.

The navigator, or teacher, of this voyage must be fit for the task, or he or she will jeopardize the lives of all on board. In other words, as much as the teacher is "determined to prepare [his or her] students for deep learning, as their teacher, [we] must prepare [ourselves] for deep learning about both teaching and learning" (Teaiwa, 2011, p. 217).

Much can be said about the ramifications of this teaching metaphor, but perhaps one of the important realities is that "without a crew there would be no major or ocean-going canoe voyage." If our students are truant or have dropped out of school altogether, how can they explore the majesty of the wide expanse of wonder?

Changing the metaphors with which we view education is a monumental task. For most of us, we have sat through 15,000 hours of classroom time before graduating from high school. Most of this time was spent subconsciously observing how teaching and learning operate. Undoing all that has been engrained in us may actually take a journey of discovery, one step at a time, around the world.

Fortunately, all we have learned about the human brain suggests that we can unravel our faulty metaphors and replace them with new, better ones. Even more fortunate are we who are not computers. For we can wonder about our predicament, think about it, grapple with it, use our imagination and creativity (what's left of it), and help our students do the same. Together, we can invite our truants to take their place alongside us, and we alongside them, on the voyage of discovery.

The problems that are spread throughout our education system have thrown the system out of balance, and homeostasis is the restoring of equilibrium. In reality, truancy is a form of homeostasis. Bad schooling and dissatisfaction with lessons produce various homeostatic responses, for example, truancy, private schooling, charter schools, home school, and replacement of poor teachers, to name a few.

These behaviors, especially truancy, are a sober response to the curriculum and pedagogy that have infiltrated our schools. Shute contends that the educational society must stop making superficial alterations to the metaphor. "These kinds of alterations are akin to straightening deck chairs of the Titanic. School attendance, I'm afraid, is hardly the core of our educational problems. The cause of these problems has always been much more basic—it is a question of metaphor, pure and simple, reliance on a wrong metaphor. We can continue to press for increased attendance at school, but that will profit us little. Until we get back to what schools should truly be about, only superficial reform will occur whilst the educational ship continues to sink. Indeed, our entire civilization may be in jeopardy" (Shute, 1994, p. 25).

REFERENCES

Balz, D. (2005, February 27). Gates says U.S. high schools ripe for reform. *Miami Herald*, p. 11A.

Coulson, A. J. (2004, May 4). Fulfilling a promise: A plan for bringing educational freedom and excellence to all Oklahomans. *Oklahoma Council of Public Affairs*.

Herbold, R. J. (2005). K–12 establishment is putting America's industrial leadership at risk. *Imprimis, 34*(5).

Murphy, J. (1990). *The educational reform movement of the 1980's: Perspective and cases*. Berkeley, CA: McCutchan Publishing Corporation.

Shute, R. W. (1994, spring). The might of metaphor: School attendance and a utilitarian view of education. *Social Work in Education*.

Teaiwa, T. (2011). Preparation for deep learning. *The Journal of Pacific History*, 46(2), 214–220, DOI: 10.1080/00223344.2011.607269.

Yero, J. L. (2010). *Teaching in mind: How teacher thinking shapes education*. Hamilton, MT: MindFlight Publishing.

Zhao, Y. (2012). *World class learners: Educating creative and entrepreneurial students*. Thousand Oaks, CA: Corwin Press.

Chapter Nine

A Good Teacher

To say that teaching is a demanding job would be an understatement. However, teachers persist because at some level we care about the well-being and learning of children and youth. Of course, better pay would also help, but seeing the learning progress, our students' eyes light up with a creative idea or contribution, and the focus on their faces when they are engrossed in a personally meaningful project bring a certain contentment that is its own reward.

However, most teachers in the profession will quickly admit that the reality of being a teacher is much more than the traditional concept that teaching entails. Being a teacher is also being a surrogate parent, a referee, a judge, a therapist, a psychologist, a role model, an advocate, a cheer-leader, a coach, and many other roles.

Not only do teachers have multiple roles, they have multiple variables happening around them at the same time. Consider the following description of teaching:

Classroom teaching is not brain surgery; teaching is far more complex. Brain surgery involves—with assistance—(a) studying a patient's symptoms and determining the need for surgery, (b) specifying what the surgery is to accomplish, (c) planning for the surgical procedure, (d) preparing for the surgery (e.g., sterilizing the tools and scheduling the operating facility), (e) conducting the surgery and monitoring the patient's progress, [and] (f) evaluating the outcome of the operation. Your work as a classroom teacher is conducted in cycles that parallel the stages of brain surgery. However, unlike the brain surgeon, you do not have the luxury of working with only one client (i.e., student or patient) at a time. Typically, a teacher deals with about 30 students at a time. Whereas the brain surgeon only engages in one surgery at a time, focusing on one aspect of the patient (e.g., removing an intra-axial neoplasmic tumor from the occipital lobe) while others (e.g., an anesthesiologist) monitor variables (e.g., the patient's respiratory rate), the teacher—usually with no assistance—is expected to concurrently engage in numerous teaching cycles with about 30 students while monitoring myriad variables (e.g., self-image, aptitude, motivation, achievement, attention level, interest in the lesson's content, progress toward long-range goals, success with moment-to-moment objectives, and on/off-task behavior). Teaching is an extremely complex art. (Cangelosi, 2008, p. 4)

We would like to make two additions to the aforementioned description of teaching: (1) a brain surgeon is usually working on someone physically immobile, relaxed, and under some anesthetic, and (2) make no mistake— a teacher is working on multiple students' brains at the same time. The tragic part of teaching is that when teachers make mistakes, or become lackadaisical and burned out, the result, while tragic, is not as readily apparent as a mistake in brain surgery.

The fact is, however, that the research tells us that students don't *want* to be in school or class, not because they don't *like* school, but because they don't like what is happening at/in school. O'Keeffe points out that the data "clearly confound the view that truancy is due to factors over which schools have little or no control. If lessons were better regarded by truants, levels of truancy would fall" (O'Keeffe, 1993, p. 55).

The reasons for truancy vary from school officials and students. School officials, as we have mentioned, cite sociological outside-of-school issues, such as family, friends, poverty, and drugs. On the other hand, students have cited boredom, relationships with teachers, and useless lessons as reasons for truancy.

This dichotomy is not a new discovery. "In one survey, students cited boredom and loss of interest in school, irrelevant courses, suspensions, and bad relationships with teachers as the major factors in their decision to skip school. On the other hand, most of the school staff believed truancy to be related primarily to student problems with family and peers" (DeKalb, 1999, p. 1). Of course a student's definition of boredom may differ from a teacher's definition; however, the fact that the truant *perceives* the lesson as boring and useless should be what matters to fixing truancy.

We acknowledge, again, that in making this claim, we may offend some teachers. This is not our intent. Thoughtful, well-meaning teachers put in untold hours of time and energy into the development of our nation's youth. These thoughtful, devoted teachers and educators are true heroes, which our youth continue to need, but who our education system continues to devalue by imposing more and more policies and demands on them.

Conversely, thoughtful, devoted teachers continually search for better ways to improve their craft, which sometimes creates a bit of angst as we reflect on the reality of the situation. By the word angst, we mean "a strong feeling of being worried or nervous; a feeling of anxiety about your life or situation" (merriam-webster.com).

We do have hope for conquering our educational anxieties and, therefore, our truancy problems. This chapter focuses on what teachers can do by way of better teaching and better student-teacher relationships as a way to embrace the truancy challenge and invite our students back to school.

The call for more student engagement has sounded for a number of years. Although research has not substantiated the connection between student engagement and truancy, per se, logically, the connection is clear. If students are invited and engaged, they will more likely remain at school. Teachers are the key.

However, the reality is that with ever-increasing pressure to raise student achievement on test scores, teachers are overwhelmed with a seemingly endless list of responsibilities and duties. Student absences do not rank high on the priority list. Sadly, in some cases, teachers often breathe a sigh of relief and look forward to a pleasant day when certain students are absent. Fortunately, for teachers, however, the very keys that will unlock the classroom door for these truants and engage them in learning will also greatly enhance the learning of all students, truants and nontruants alike.

Over the past many decades, literally thousands of books and journal articles have been written on effective teaching and student-teacher relationships. We have only chosen a few of these to support the idea that more engaging, effective teaching will, in fact, lessen the truancy problem and bring our students back to school.

Teachers share the blame for truancy because their lessons are unengaging. Their methods are based on faulty metaphors, which we discussed at length in the previous chapter. As we have asserted throughout this book, teachers and lessons impact truancy. "The most important factor affecting student learning is the teacher" (Marzano et al., 2003, p. 1).

In order to understand what a better lesson is, we must understand what an effective teacher does because "seemingly more can be done to improve education by improving the effectiveness of teachers than by any other single factor" (Marzano et al., 2003, p. 1). Research shows that effective teachers greatly impact student achievement.

Effective teachers can expect to see gains of 52 percentile points in student achievement over one year while the least effective teachers will see student achievement gains of 14 percentile points, which includes 6 percentile points of maturation gains (Marzano et al., 2003, p. 2)! Marzano's research also shows that effective teaching, even in schools considered to be "bad" schools, will see better student achievement (63 percentile points over two years) than ineffective teaching in "good" schools (37 percentile points over two years) (p. 3). We know effective teaching matters.

We know effective teaching is critical to our present study toward trumping truancy; we assert that truancy rates will decline as effective teaching efforts increase. To achieve better teaching and better lessons, three functions are inseparably connected in order for effective teachers to create better lessons.

1. All effective teachers must make wise choices regarding the most effective instructional strategies to use. This includes being skilled at using cooperative learning, graphic organizers, homework, and questions.
2. Effective teachers must design curriculum in a way that facilitates student learning. This includes identifying and using the proper sequence and pacing. In other words, teachers should not solely rely on the scope and sequence stated in textbooks but should be able to consider the individual and collective needs of their students, using a wide variety of learning activities in different formats (i.e., stories, presentations, media).
3. Effective teachers must make effective and skillful classroom management decisions. (Marzano et al., 2003, p. 3)

Unfortunately, research has shown that the following negative teacher behaviors exist in classrooms relating to teaching: "absenteeism [*teacher*], tardiness [*teacher*], keeping students overtime, early dismissal, straying from the subject matter, being unprepared or unorganized, being late returning work" (Marzano et al., 2003, pp. 32–33; italics added). With these teacher behaviors and others happening in the classroom, we understand how rational students would leave that classroom.

Effective teaching is also engaged teaching (Weaver & Wilding, 2013). Brain research supports the call for engaged teaching (Bransford, Brown, & Cocking, 2000; Jensen, 2008; Sousa, 2011). Of course thousands of books and articles focus on the aspects of engaged teaching and using brain science to facilitate deeper learning.

We know that emotional states, physical movement, physical environment, social interactions, critical thinking, novelty, and reflection are all extremely critical for deep learning (Jensen, 2005). Our lessons and practice must align with the research.

According to truancy research, students intuitively know good from bad lessons, and good from bad teachers. "If classes are oppressive, dull, and unchallenging, students are provoked to cry out and complain. They may passively resist in class or students may choose not to attend certain classes at all" (Guare & Cooper, 2003, p. 79).

In addition to effective teaching, teachers must become better classroom managers. Marzano states, and we agree, that "effective teaching and learning cannot take place in a poorly managed classroom" (2003, p. 1).

Being a better classroom manager starts with the ability to build positive teacher-student relationships. As a whole, effective classroom management is the ability to provide a positive learning environment that is safe and conducive to student learning. In addition to effective teaching, other components make up classroom management: student-teacher relationships, discipline, mental set, rules, and procedures. Each of these parts plays a critical role in the success of school, and all of these components are inextricably woven together.

We assert that applying a few key classroom management principles, in addition to effective teaching, will greatly improve the learning environment and subsequently reduce truancy. As a whole, effective classroom management is the ability to provide a positive learning environment that is safe and conducive to student learning.

Teacher-student relationships are, perhaps, the foundation of a positive learning environment, as well as the foundation upon which classroom management is built. "Our ability to learn has deep roots in relationships. Our learning performance may be deeply affected by the emotional environment in which learning takes place" (quoted in Weaver & Wilding, 2013, p. 9).

If positive student-teacher relationships flourish in the classroom, students are more likely to attend, abide by the rules and expectations, be receptive to the corrective process, and complete projects. In fact, "many behavioral problems ultimately boil down to a breakdown in teacher-student relationships" (Marzano et al., 2003, p. 42).

Positive teacher-student relationships affect both students and teachers. Teachers feel better about arriving at school, teaching in their classrooms, and helping students succeed. Conversely, students feel better about arriving at school, learning in their classrooms, and interacting with their teachers.

In other words, positive teacher-student relationships are important not only to the teacher's sanity and peace but also to the student's sanity and peace. Imagine how we feel at the end of yet another day of stress and conflicts toward those certain students who seem to get the best of us. After those days (and we have all had them), we don't feel very energetic toward teaching and school.

By projecting ourselves into a student's role, we can sense how a student might feel after yet another day of stress and conflicts with *us*, and at the middle school and high school levels, students feel this way with six or seven teachers.

Needless to say, positive relationships are important to teachers *and* students. Of course solving relationship problems is the focus of innumerable therapists and psychologists. Look into the eyes of our students, and the thoughtful teacher will understand the inescapable reality that they must be proactive in relationships with their students if they want their day to be smooth and learning to take place. In our study of truancy, however, teachers must understand that their relationships with their students are completely their responsibility.

Our research and other research have uncovered that students truant to escape what is happening in the classroom. Truants have cited perceived prejudice, insults, sarcasm, and rudeness as reasons for their truancy (Guare & Cooper, 2003; O'Keeffe, 1993; Shute, 2009).

Research shows that other certain teacher behaviors, in regard to student-teacher relationships, are prevalent in classrooms. These are the following: sarcasm and put-downs, verbal abuse, unreasonable and arbitrary rules, lack of response to student questions, sexual harassment, apathy toward students, negative personality, showing favoritism, straying from the subject matter, being unprepared or unorganized (Marzano et al., 2003, p. 33).

In this regard, we must also acknowledge that some teachers *are* directly at fault for driving away our students. Ask any group of college students to tell you about their experiences with schoolteachers. While positive and uplifting stories will be shared, horror stories will also begin to surface.

We have heard of teachers who rip up tests in front of third graders and harshly demand that they take the test over. We have personally heard teachers swearing at students, yelling in frustration, and lashing out with rude remarks. We have seen teachers who exhibit a detached demeanor, go through the day full of impatience—the list goes on.

"These kinds of reactions virtually never remediate a situation. . . . This approach encourages students to want to escape what should otherwise be a positive experience" (Latham, 1998, p. 25). Brief self-reflection will remind us that we do not like this behavior when it is directed at us.

In the words of Murray Sidman, "We react to coercion by avoiding or escaping from our coercers if we can. . . . Millions of pupils would escape from school immediately if the law permitted" (Latham, 1998, p. 25). This exodus from our schools and teachers is occurring in the form of truancy. Many teachers have seemingly forgotten the joy that teaching can bring.

One way of describing teacher-student relationships is with a quadrant diagram (see figure 9.1). At the top end of the vertical line separating the quadrant, we put high dominance and opposite, on the bottom end, is high submission. On the horizontal line dividing the quadrant, we put high cooperation on the extreme right and high opposition opposite on the extreme left.

A teacher who has a high level of dominance would be characterized as having clarity of purpose and strong guidance, academically and behaviorally. While these are positive characteristics, the extreme of high dominance leads to lack of attentiveness to the students and concern for their interests. Opposite of high dominance is high submission, which is a lack of clarity and purpose.

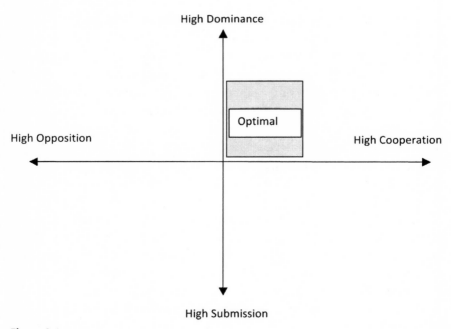

Figure 9.1.

A balance between the two is optimal. The horizontal line of the quadrant depicts the spectrum of high cooperation to high opposition. High cooperation can be characterized by a deep "concern for the needs and opinions of others and a desire to function as a member of a team as opposed to an individual" (Marzano et al., 2003, p. 43).

These are positive traits, but extreme cooperation is an "inability or lack of resolve to act without the input and approval of others. Extreme opposition—the other end of this continuum—is characterized by active antagonism toward others and a desire to thwart their goals and desires" (Marzano et al., 2003, p. 43).

Remember our purpose here is to relate these to *teacher* behavior. Optimal student-teacher relationships are a balance between high dominance and high cooperation. See figure 9.1 (adapted from Marzano et al., 2003, p. 43).

A good overall description of good teacher characteristics is that teachers "should be able to empathize with students, understand their world, and listen to them. Good teachers are not uncertain, undecided, or confusing in the way they communicate with students. They are not grouchy, gloomy, dissatisfied, aggressive, sarcastic, or quick-tempered" (Marzano et al., 2003, p. 44).

Another critical characteristic of good teachers is the ability to instill confidence in their students. We have all heard this, but in practice the very subtle clues we give students do not instill confidence. One way to avoid these subtle clues is not to automatically assume something is deficient in the students when achievement outcomes are not met. "When students had difficulty in class, the best [teachers] looked for problems in their courses first rather than in their students' preparation or intelligence" (Bain, 2010, p. 78).

As teachers develop the trait of being able to look inward first, they are more likely to exude an air of confidence toward their students: " . . . the best teaching can be found not in particular practices or rules but in the *attitudes* of the teachers, in their *faith* in their students' abilities to achieve, in their *willingness* to take their students seriously and to let them assume control of their own education, and in their *commitment* to let all policies and practices flow from central learning objectives and from a mutual respect and agreement between students and teachers" (Bain, 2010, pp. 78–79; original italics).

In other words, every interaction we have with students sends a message.

> We consider every behavior that someone displays in the presence of someone else as a communication, and therefore we assume that in the presence of someone else one cannot *not* communicate. . . . Whatever someone's intentions are, the other persons in the communication will infer meaning from that someone's behavior. If, for example, teachers ignore students' questions, perhaps because they do not hear them, then students may not only get this inattention but also infer that the teacher is too busy or thinks that the students are too dull to understand or that the questions are impertinent. The message that students take from the teacher's negation can be different from the teacher's intention. (Marzano et al., 2003, p. 49; original italics)

Of course blatant teacher and student behaviors also exist. The behavior of purposely ignoring students and using threats, criticism, arguments, sarcasm, and force are never worthwhile.

It is not this book's purpose to be a classroom management manual covering all the necessary information to be a successful, effective teacher. Nor is it intended to offer strategies to solve discipline problems. Many

wonderful, research-based discipline approaches exist to help all teachers (e.g., Lee Canter's *Assertive Discipline*, William Glasser's *Choice
Theory*, Fred Jones's *Positive Discipline*, Jim Fay's *Love and Logic*,
and many others). Each approach should not be considered a cure for all
problems but each contains pieces that can be adapted by all teachers and
effective with all students.

This book does, however, aim to help teachers understand that the
power to invite students back to class is manifested in their relationships
with their students. By way of caution, any positive change takes time.
Creating a good teacher-student relationship is a skill. Responding to
students in an appropriate way is a skill and like other skills must be practiced to become automatic.

Latham suggests that teachers should identify the situations where they
are most likely to become frustrated and negative, describe those situations in writing, script a positive response, and practice the response in
the environment where the behavior occurs (the classroom, even at their
student's desk) at least 30 to 40 times. One may feel foolish and awkward,
but with practice, these positive interaction skills will become automatic.

Of course there is a strong likelihood that you will make mistakes and
revert back to negative behaviors. When this happens, apologize and
move on. And, of course, we must remember that

> in the process of putting positive teacher-to-pupil interactions to work, situ-
> ations will arise which will so annoy you or so unnerve you that your mind
> just goes blank relative to the use of positive strategies. The inclination to be
> reactive and negative . . . comes flooding over you. In such an instance, when
> you can't think of an appropriate way of responding and you're overwhelmed
> with an urge to react and to be negative, don't do anything. Remember this
> admonition: Unless what you are about to say or do has a high probability
> for making things better, don't say it and don't do it. . . . Before reacting wait
> until your wits are about you or until you are able to review your notes and
> practice a more appropriate way of responding. In the meantime, redirect your
> behavior to other things that must be done. (Latham, 1998, pp. 57–58)

An education survey was recently released showing results from what
is known as the Educator Effectiveness System. The survey was completed by 171,180 students in fall 2013 to evaluate 9,659 teachers. Seven
teacher characteristics were measured. Table 9.1 shows the percentages
of teachers who scored "favorably" in each of the seven characteristics.

Table 9.1.   Educator Effectiveness System fall 2013 results.

Teacher Characteristic	% of Teachers Who Scored Favorably (# of teachers) n=9659
Care: Show concern and commitment	49% (4,733)
Challenge: Press for rigor and persistence	67% (6,472)
Captivate: Inspire curiosity and interest	53% (5,119)
Confer: Invite ideas and promote discussion	47% (4,540)
Consolidate: Integrate ideas and check for understanding	59% (5,699)
Control: Sustain order, respect and focus	47% (4,540)
Clarify: Cultivate understanding and overcome confusion	61% (5,892)

Adapted from Kalani, N. (2014, February 22). Students tell how teachers measure up. *Star Advertiser*, p. A1, A7.

Controversy abounds over this latest effort to measure teachers. "The student surveys are designed to evaluate seven elements of teaching practices that correspond to teaching quality" (Kalani, 2014, p. A1). Personal decisions, including pay increases, tenure, and termination will be tied to the survey results. In the state of Hawaii, and other states, many teachers (84%) object to letting the students have a part in the decision of their pay and tenure (p. A7). Many teachers claim that the students may have difficulty understanding the wording of the questions and, therefore, be unable to answer them reliably.

While these concerns are valid, if the results are even marginally accurate, a lot of teachers are not perceived as being very good teachers by the students who are entrusted to them. Table 9.1 shows that control (the ability to sustain order, respect, and focus), confer (inviting ideas and promoting discussion), and care (showing concern and commitment) are the lowest areas with 47%, 47%, and 49%, respectively.

In other words, when our students go to school each day, they are going into classrooms where they perceive that the teacher does not show concern or commitment to them, where the teacher does not sustain order, respect, and focus, and where their ideas are not promoted. Granted, these are the students' perceptions, but we all want our perceptions to be valued.

The preceding paragraphs may have appeared to be negative toward teachers. Our purpose has been to point out that teachers wield amazing influence, perhaps more than is readily perceptible, over our students. The logical connection is that our students are truanting as a rational decision to escape from classes they judge to be useless and teachers who they judge to be unfit.

REFERENCES

Bain, Ken (2004). *What the Best College Teachers Do*. Cambridge, MA. Harvard University Press.

Bransford, J. D., Brown, A. L., & Cocking, R. R. (Eds.). (2000). *How people learn: Brain, mind, experience, and school*. Washington, D.C.: National Academy Press.

Cangelosi, J. S. (2008). *Classroom management strategies: Gaining and maintaining students' cooperation*. 6th ed. Hoboken, NJ: John Wiley & Sons, Inc.

DeKalb, J. (1999). *Student truancy*. U.S. Department of Education. ERIC, ED429334.

Guare, R., & Cooper, B. S. (2003). *Truancy revisited: Students as school consumers*. Lanham, MD: Scarecrow Press, Inc.

Jensen, E. (2005). *Teaching with the brain in mind*. Alexandria, VA: Association for Supervision and Curriculum Development (ASCD).

Jensen, E. (2008). *Brain-based learning: The new paradigm of teaching*. Thousand Oaks, CA: Corwin Press.

Kalani, N. (2014, February 22). Students tell how teachers measure up. *Star Advertiser*, p. A1, A7.

Latham, G. I. (1998). *Keys to classroom management*. North Logan, UT: P & T Ink.

Marzano, R. J., with Marzano, J. S. & Pickering, D. J. (2003). *Classroom management that works: Research-based strategies for every teacher*. Alexandria, VA: Association for Supervision and Curriculum Development (ASCD).

Merriam-webster.com. www.merriam-webster.com/dictionary/angst (accessed June 13, 2014).

O'Keeffe, D. (1993). *Truancy in English secondary schools: A report prepared for the DFE*. London: HMSO.

Shute, J. W. (2009). *Expanding the truancy debate: Truancy, ethnic minorities and English language learners*. In M. Conolly and D. O'Keeffe (Eds.), *Don't Fence Me In: Essays on the Rational Truant* (pp. 115–38). Buckingham, England: The University of Buckingham Press.

Sousa, D. A. (2011). *How the brain learns*. Thousand Oaks, CA: Corwin Press.

Weaver, L., & Wilding, M. (2013). *The five dimensions of engaged teaching: A practical guide for educators*. Bloomington, IN: Solution Tree Press.

Chapter Ten

Fixing Truancy

Truancy, the act of intentionally absenting oneself from class or school, is a colossal problem with a serious detrimental impact on our students, teachers, and resources. Research suggests that missing class after arriving at school occurs far more often than missing entire days of school. The implication is that students, for the most part, are not rebelling against education, rather against what is happening in some classrooms.

The traditional view of truancy would claim that these truants are juvenile delinquents and devious youth who are turning their backs on education. Research now shows that while some truants fit this profile, the vast majority are rational decision-makers who are disappointed in what the classroom has to offer. This being the case, we must explore the option that curriculum and pedagogy, teachers and administrators, are partially to blame.

In fairness to teachers and the school system, perhaps some few students are not suited to schooling. These students have no interest, their parents have little participation, and no matter how engaging or interesting the ways in which the lessons are presented, these students will only be biding their time until they can be free from the constraints of school. What to do with these students is a subject that needs study beyond the scope of this project.

However, the surprising results of numerous truancy studies make it impossible to place all, or even most, of truanting children, whether Caucasian or minority, in such a category. The following steps need taking to focus our efforts on fixing truancy now.

REDEFINING TRUANCY

As has been sufficiently asserted in the previous pages of this book, truancy in America, in general, and specifically among minorities, with all of its various ramifications, desperately needs to be viewed differently. The enormous number of children truanting each day in American schools demands a fresh redefinition of the term "truancy" so that it does not conjure up in the minds of people the idea that the majority of truanting students are delinquent or engaging in criminal behavior.

A redefinition is desperately needed because, as we have found, students tend to truant from specific classes after they have arrived at school. After including class truancy in the definition, we can more reliably classify truants as chronic truants, habitual truants, or truants and further classify them as predominantly class truants or school truants within these categories.

The great majority of truanting children are not those who cut entire days of school but rather those who choose to skip specific classes once they have arrived on the school grounds. Since this is the case, cutting class must be included in the truancy definition, which means we must also include class cutting in our truancy prevention efforts, which would then bring us back to evaluating what is happening in our classrooms.

None of what we are saying implies that school truancy is not also a huge, expensive, and wasteful problem. But the evidence suggests that class truancy takes place more often than school truancy.

LOOK INWARD

After a redefinition of the word truancy is firmly set in the minds of educators, administrators, and policy-makers, we must elevate the intellectual location of truancy as a subject for scholarly enquiry. As we reflect on the amazing incidences of truancy taking place, we naturally ask the overall question, "Why?" Obviously, huge numbers of students do not want to be in class and do not feel that being there is necessary. The widespread nature of the problem seems to indicate fundamental and profound causes.

Evidence suggests that students do not hate school. Most students, including most truants, like school. In other words, the evidence suggests that while other variables are without question at work, truancy, if viewed as a barometer of successful education, connects mostly to curriculum and pedagogy. We must recognize that truancy, like education, relates above all to curriculum and pedagogy.

The students we are talking about have very clear notions of what constitutes good and bad lessons and good and bad teaching. If we view truancy as an indication of a problem with curriculum and pedagogy, we can better support our teachers who are working hard but fighting a losing battle without support where needed.

The astonishingly high level of truancy makes it painfully clear that a huge number of children, while valuing education, do not see the necessity and value of their particular classes or feel the satisfaction meaningful learning can bring. These students pick and choose the classes they want to attend. Does it not stand to reason that if what happened in the classroom were different, the children might behave differently?

Missing specific classes is arguably a deliberate choice on the part of a majority of truanting children, calculated not as a deviant behavior but as a rational choice to do something they feel is more relevant and satisfying to them than sitting in a specific classroom.

When administrators, curriculum writers, and policy-makers eventually come to the realization that class truancy is an even larger category of truancy than school truancy, the solutions for this acute problem can be more honestly attacked and effective solutions more likely found. Surely the curriculum (and all that this term means), with its attendant pedagogical arrangements, must form a bigger part of the truancy picture. Until this is understood, school leaders continue to blame others for this malfunction rather than looking inward for solutions.

Another critical way school administrators and leaders can directly help fix the truancy problem is by being honest and open in getting to the heart of the problem rather than fearing and covering up the problem of truancy. Surely there should not be resistance to studies about truancy by those whose background and experience can be helpful. Education, after all, is the pursuit of learning, yet studies on truancy encounter a great deal of resistance.

This suggests that many educational leaders are not interested in learning more about this problem. Administrators should work with school teachers, parent groups, student groups, and interested agencies in an open manner to realize that the truancy problem may be a problem within the school itself.

SUPPORT

In addition to viewing truancy differently, school administrators and policy-makers must support school instructional personnel and curriculum leaders in understanding that old beliefs about truancy are no longer valid. Truancy, as we have shown, is not engaged in, for the most part, by deviant children but rather by rational children who make a decision to cut classes that they feel are irrelevant or to escape the classroom or school with which they are not satisfied or feel threatened. In much of the literature on truancy, changes to the school curriculum and pedagogy are rarely considered as a way to curb truancy.

Yet, studies show that boredom, loss of interest, and irrelevant courses have been found to be major factors contributing to truancy (Chesney-Lind et al., 2004; DeKalb, 1999; Roderick et al., 1997). The data suggest that many current curriculum and pedagogy arrangements are not very appealing to young people.

In addition, teacher education and curriculum issues should be adapted more and more to the needs of an increasingly larger population of ethnic minority children. This is especially true for students for whom English is a second language, students who obviously need a more meaningful and engaging environment in school than they are currently experiencing.

Unfortunately, many teachers are required, or allowed, to teach subjects about which they have no profound knowledge or scholarship, often subjects in which they themselves have little interest. They must teach with the goal of helping the children pass boring, meaningless, standardized tests.

Classrooms are overcrowded so that needed individual attention is difficult. Writing assignments that would help children learn to think and express their thoughts coherently are impossible to carefully correct, even if the teachers' writing skills were such that they were able to do so.

Textbooks hold no adventure, no imagination, and no spirit of inquiry in the dreary process of studying from them. In our system, teachers learn methods instead of substance. They learn how to teach but have no deep or profound knowledge of what should be taught. In our system, the teacher sadly becomes a babysitter. Truanting children choose not to be babysat. Logically, we must look at curriculum and pedagogy arrangements as possible solutions if we are going to solve this colossal problem.

ENGLISH LANGUAGE CENTERS

We might also further consider the problem of language facility and its relationship to truancy. American schools are taught in the English language. Whether English is a first or second language does not, in and of itself, determine the individual child's mastery of English. As we all know, many English-speaking children are nearly illiterate—they cannot read or write with even minimal competency, and many English language learners are highly literate and successful.

When we consider the problem of truancy as related to language skills, we might ask: what is the correlation between truancy and competent, or even scholarly, mastery of the English language?

Whether speaking English or another language as their first language, do students who have mastery of English in reading and writing truant less often than those whose reading and writing skills are poor? Does poor language facility among the Caucasian students underlie much of their truancy? Logically, a child who does not have excellent language skills, whether Caucasian or minority, will not have the proper foundation for meeting the challenges of his educational world and will be discouraged and frustrated by school.

Perhaps the key to solving the truancy problem in America lies in teaching English as the priority subject, realizing that reading ability is the key to all learning. For all students, Caucasian or minority, perhaps language—reading and writing at a high, even scholarly level of proficiency—should be required before any other classes are attempted.

Peripheral subjects like history, social studies, and science classes should only be taken after language proficiency is gained. Any student who speaks, reads, and writes the English language on a scholarly level is prepared to gain any knowledge he desires, inside or outside of university, whereas a child who has poor language skills and has fumbled through high school classes by whatever means possible has little educational foundation at all, even though he may hold a diploma in his hand.

The educational community must focus efforts to fix truancy among all minority groups, including English language learners. As has been shown, this population of students, immigrants and nonimmigrants, has and continues to grow rapidly. As this growth continues, these students must be given opportunities to succeed at a different level than their English-as-a-first-language peers. Research shows that language facility is related to truancy. As we have pointed out, whether English is a first or second language does not, in and of itself, determine the individual child's mastery of English.

Students' perception of their English language ability, whether it be speaking, reading, writing, or listening, does indeed have an effect on their propensity to truant.

This being the case, we recommend that English language centers be established in high schools to allow ELL students to improve their language ability and to be integrated into the mainstream of learning when they have an optimal grasp on English, a grasp that will propel them into a successful educational experience. This is not to lower the expectation that the schools should have toward minority children but to simply level the playing field so they can succeed.

English language centers exist at virtually every college and university in the United States to accommodate English language learners and English language deficiencies. Our contention is that if research shows language learning is more optimal at an early age, why are we not providing intensive support in upper elementary, middle, and high schools? This kind of arrangement, if considered creatively and thoughtfully, could succeed also at the elementary and secondary school levels.

College and university ethnic minority students who speak English as a second language attend English language centers until their proficiency is at a level where they can succeed in the university. Yet, in high school we have students struggling and failing as a result of low English language proficiency and with surprisingly little help available to them.

Politics and money are always involved. However, as the problem of truancy lessens, more students are obviously back in school and more funding is provided to the schools. As our nation spends money on truancy programs that actually work, more students are back in school, and the millions of dollars a day being forfeited across the country can be used to fund centers such as the ones suggested.

POLICIES AND IMPLEMENTATION

The data suggest that most students believe that their schools have strict attendance policies and that the policies will be enforced. However, students continue to truant in large numbers. It is clear, then, that something is wrong with the implementation of the policies and regulations. Preventions that involve truancy officers, probation officers, and police officers continue to put pressure on truants without lasting change to improving education and student achievement. As we continue to crack down on truants, students will continue to flaunt the law and give the rules only minimal attention.

Along with the changes proposed earlier, a complete review of the truancy policies should be conducted in an effort to cull out those that are inappropriate to keep and maintain those that are appropriate. If we are serious as a society to have truancy rules and regulations, and they are appropriate for the benefit of the students, and they represent the realities we have discussed in this book, then they should be implemented properly and enforced. Otherwise, they are a sham and of little value in helping youngsters gain a worthy education.

Government officials must set informed laws that are compatible with what we are proposing here. In addition, parents must be involved in shaping the rules pertaining to truancy, and, as we will state later, we advocate that students should be involved with prevention efforts.

School-wide improvement of truancy policies requires a basic infrastructure to support teachers' efforts to improve attendance, such as information systems, smaller and more personalized instruction environments, clearly defined policies, and support services (Roderick et al., 1997, p. 12). This also means personalized attendance monitoring to identify early school truants, class truants, and habitual tardiness.

Most teachers will agree that a disconnect exists between their attendance efforts related to truancy and near truancy and actual action taken by administrations. Typically, teachers identify daily tardy and absent students. Periodically, they wonder what the administration is doing, because feedback on actions taken is rarely communicated. Conversely, administrators are already short on time as they are bombarded with other pressing matters. Attending to the truancy problem is temporarily set aside until extreme cases surface.

One problem that administrators face is the reality of what to do with truants. Letters are sent home with no response in some cases. Legal action is taken in some cases. Often students and parents ignore the court action or end up back in school to satisfy justice only for the student to truant again when the legal pressure subsides. The cycle starts again after a few months. Eventually, the truant either drops out altogether, ends up in jail for other criminal behavior, or completes school and has "moved on" from being a school problem. Then, another extreme truancy case emerges.

When we examine the premises upon which our educational system is built, the first reality we have to face is that those who plan the curriculum and train the teachers are far removed from the lives of the students. To change that system is very nearly impossible because those who make the decisions in any institution become a law unto themselves. We have indicated that most truant children are not delinquent and deviant children but ordinary children caught in a system that they find difficult to tolerate.

Many reasons abound for our system's deterioration, but most of them stem from a lack of local control. Regulations that show a lack of faith in able and competent teachers and administrators, responsible parents, and motivated students continue to suppress and smother any spark of hope for lasting and solid reform in education. Without these changes, the staggering illiteracy and innumeracy rates among our children who are "dumbed down" ever lower and lower, year after year, will continue to worsen.

STUDENT INVOLVEMENT

We know that students truant from class and school. Sadly, this phenomenon starts early. "Children abandon schools in the second grade attitudinally and in the tenth grade physically, not because they are stupid but because they don't care. They have been estranged from school" (Cooper, 1998, p. 3).

In a broad sense, schools should operate on the same sound principles as any other free-market enterprise or free civil association. Choice for education is imperative and essential to the learning interests of students. Many students, quite frankly, are not engaged in learning, nor do they appear interested in becoming so under our current system.

Cooper explains, that "students are the schools' clients. When kids skip these services, it is time to ask why: 'You skipped my class yesterday. Did you have a personal problem, or is my course boring?'" (Cooper, 1998, p. 3). At present, students' lack of involvement and the persistent "us-against-them" mentality has led to a lackadaisical effort among our young people.

A hunger and thirst for education is alien to many of them. Creativity and critical thinking have been smothered as students sit in a class they don't want to be in. Tragically, truly motivated students are the ones who suffer as the system caters to unmotivated students and parents. If choice were to be given to students, they and their parents would be much more likely to put school as a high priority in their lives.

Truancy is a clear indication of how truants feel toward school and, more particularly, class. To produce the long-lasting, positive changes to the truancy problem, students must be involved. Guare and Cooper suggest the following: "Listen to the students. Seeking to understand students' points of view and valuing their perspectives are essential to creating meaningful school communities. Alienation and disengagement from learning are all too common experiences for students" (Guare & Cooper, 2003, p. 79).

Interestingly, "boredom, loss of interest in school, suspensions, irrelevant courses, and bad relationships with teachers is cause for truancy" have all been stated reasons why students truant (Chesney-Lind et al., 2004, p. 46). Simply put, "students remark that school is a dull and boring, nonengaging environment . . ." (Sousa, 2011, p. 34).

Other reasons are "absence of educational goals, lack of stimulation for students, [and] neglect of diverse student needs." All of these reasons could be addressed if students were involved in the process. Guare and Cooper continue: "Engage students in anti-truancy efforts. Measures should be taken to discuss classes and courses with students. What can I do to make my algebra class more interesting to you? What bores you?" (Guare & Cooper, 2003, p. 84).

As students feel an investment in school and feel involved in the education process in meaningful ways, they will want to attend. As one author writes, "How do we solve the truancy problem? Make sure that schools meet basic needs for respect, control, and competence . . . better than street gangs" (Fay & Fay, 2001, p. 8).

Being educators, these researchers admit that children, by reasons of their inexperience, are not in all things capable of making decisions to determine what is best for their lives. Allowing them complete freedom in their choices of school courses is not a responsible solution for the long-term benefit of our youth, which, of course, is not what we are suggesting. But students should be involved in their education, and they should have a desire to learn, and that learning should be meaningful.

As has been shown, education is viewed, for the most part, as important not only to the parents of minority children but also to the students themselves. Why then, we ask, are the truancy levels astronomically high?

By improving curriculum, pedagogy, and inviting student involvement in the process, more students will be in class and subsequently have a better chance to succeed. In short, "schools need to 'see' their students differently as though they were 'paying customers' that need to be listened to, heeded, and involved. Being conscripted to school, forced to sit through unwanted classes and experiences, and then told to enjoy it seems a triple insult" (Guare & Cooper, 2003, p. 71).

Another benefit of involving students in their education process is a developed sense of responsibility. "Young people should see school and learning as their 'job.' It builds our civic culture and prepares them for a productive adulthood. Schools do need rules and regulations on attendance, but we must recognize that such regulations alone cannot work. A sense of civic duty—a commitment to the wider culture—shifts attendance from an externally imposed obligation to an internalized, personal responsibility" (Cooper, 1998, p. 4).

HIGH EXPECTATIONS

High expectations, regardless of the extra work this may entail, must be required of our youngsters.

In our time, the proponents of "self-esteem" have apparently had their way for too long. What has become most important in our schools is the development of "self-esteem," a theme that has been elevated over high learning standards. What has happened as a result is that our children have neither good self-esteem nor a high level of educational achievement.

We declare that self-esteem is built by hard work, making the right choices, and being accountable. Our education system has made it frightfully easy to "pass;" it has practically done away with the need to make the right choices, and it has obliterated accountability at all levels. The appallingly low intellectual level of many of our children and the threat of moral decadence in our society are the results.

As we look at the problems of truanting minority children, we might profitably consider the idea of "victimhood." Minority groups have been fed a steady diet of discontent, largely through the media, to the effect that they are victims of a cruel and heartless white society that favors inexorably the majority white Caucasian populace.

As Sykes explains, there is a "new American obsession with victimhood, the pervasive lament that we are all victims and that nothing that happens to us is our fault" (Sykes, 1995, flyleaf). He goes on to say that in this kind of don't-blame-me mentality, there are obvious profound dangers. He also suggests that we must rebuild a society founded on common sense and personal responsibility.

One possible reason for the high truanting problem among minorities is that they may have, to some degree, bought into the notion that they are victims of a society that cares little for them, and to the degree that school arrangements have not been thoughtfully developed to meet their needs, this is a justified complaint. There also may be a kind of Pygmalion effect at work, in that minority students are almost "expected" to have high levels of truancy, and with this expectation their high truancy levels are self-fulfilling prophecies.

Although the vast majority of ethnic minority truants view education as valuable, they may have perhaps become disenchanted to the point where they see little value in attending school. They do not see the education they are currently receiving as a possible ticket to break the cycle of poverty, discouragement, distress, and hopelessness.

The schools have failed to uphold the vision minority parents and children once had of their potential until, finally, the vision has burned out. These minority students may see themselves as victims and not realize that this mentality is their true enemy.

The expectations that we hold out for our youngsters must be elevated. Surely, many factors come into play when we are setting expectations, but since our very civilization depends on an educated citizenry, only the highest expectations should be considered. If these expectations are not set to bring out the best in our young people, then our young people will be "dumbed down," as suggested by Sykes.

Unfortunately, by their own admission, students claim that they are not being challenged. In a "survey of 10,500 high school students conducted by the National Governors Association (2005), more than one-third of the students said their school had not done a good job challenging them to think critically and analyze problems. About 11 percent said they were thinking of dropping out of school. Over one-third of this group said they were leaving because they were 'not learning anything'" (Sousa, 2011, p. 34).

We believe that what Henry Gradillas and Jaime Escalante accomplished at Garfield High School in East Los Angeles should be promoted as the rule in education in our country rather than the exception (Mathews, 1988). Here was a group of Hispanic children attending school in East Los Angeles. They came, for the most part, from barrios of poverty and crime. But Gradillas had a dream that if the standards were set at the highest level comparable to the best high schools in the land, and the parents and the children were convinced that they had the wherewithal to achieve those standards, these Hispanic children could perform as did children from the best high schools. We must remember that East Los Angeles was, at the time, arguably one of the toughest areas in the country.

But Gradillas and Escalante were bold enough to believe that these children, like any children, would measure up to the expectations set before them—they could be the best, and, as is now well-documented history, they became the best. Escalante's math students excelled beyond a dream—they became extraordinarily good students.

At one point, it was reported that one-third of all Hispanic students who had passed advanced placement tests in the United States were from Garfield High School in East Los Angeles (Mathews, 1988). In reality, any person who really achieves has had to live up to a high expectation.

Our world is full of examples of success, all of which came about through hard work, self-discipline, accountability, and measuring up to high expectations. If schools and teachers like this exist, and we know they do, why then are not all schools following this proven pattern of success?

CONCLUSION

Truancy is a symptom of a much larger problem having to do with the way we envision learning and the way we organize ourselves to bring to pass the vision. Without a new vision and new educational arrangements, teachers, administrators, and policy-makers will always be fighting truancy. We will continue, as Thoreau said, "to simply hack away at the branches of the problem and not the roots of it."

Instead, we must embrace the truancy challenge, look inside the school for solutions to truancy, and believe in our students as rational decision-makers capable of making positive contributions to overall education systems, curriculum included. Thus we provide them real opportunities to succeed as they engage with teachers and a curriculum in a meaningful, positive, exciting learning environment—our schools.

REFERENCES

Chesney-Lind, M., et al. (2004, February). *Arrest trends, gang involvement, and truancy in Hawaii: An interim report to the twenty-second Hawaii state legislature.* Center for Youth Research, Social Science Research Institute, University of Hawaii at Manoa.

Cooper, B. S. (1998). *Skipping school for fun and profit.* Hudson Institute. Hudson.org.

DeKalb, Jay (1999). "Student Truancy." U.S. Department of Education, 1999. ERIC DIGEST, ED429334. April, 1999.

Fay, J., & Fay, C. (2001). *Love and logic teacher-isms: Wise words for teachers.* Golden, CO: The Love and Logic Institute, Inc.

Guare, R., & Cooper, B. S. (2003). *Truancy revisited: Students as school consumers.* Lanham, MD: Scarecrow Press, Inc.

Mathews, J. (1988). *Escalante: The best teacher in America.* New York: Henry Holt and Company.

Roderick, M., Arney, M., Axelman, M., DaCosta, K., Steiger, C., Stone, S., Villarreal-Sosa, L., & Waxman, E. (1997, July). Habits hard to break: A new look at truancy in Chicago's public high schools. University of Chicago. http://ccsr.uchicago.edu/sites/default/files/publications/p0a09.pdf. Retrieved March, 2014.

Sousa, D. A. (2011). *How the brain learns.* Thousand Oaks, CA: Corwin Press.

Sykes, C. J. (1992). *A nation of victims: The decay of the American character.* New York: St. Martin's Griffin.

Sykes, C. J. (1995). *Dumbing down our kids: Why America's children feel good about themselves but can't read, write, or add.* New York: St. Martin's Griffin.

Index

CPSIA information can be obtained at www.ICGtesting.com
Printed in the USA
BVOW07*0105160914

366930BV00002B/9/P